Lessons Learned
After Harvard
Business School

WISDOM SHARED BY THE
CLASS OF 1970

JEFFREY D. CHOKEL

Printed in the United States of America

First Printing, 2017

ISBN Printed book: 978-0-9980194-0-6
ePub: 978-0-9980194-1-3
ePDF: 978-0-9980194-2-0

Pinstripe Press
530 Eagle Point Drive
Lyndhurst, Ohio 44124

TABLE OF CONTENTS

About the Author

JEFF CHOKEL WENT TO PRINCETON University on a journalism scholarship and wrote articles for area newspapers as a "stringer" covering the Princeton community. During his senior year, he wrote for *The New York Times*, holding a position passed down to him by Alan Blinder, later a Princeton professor and former Vice Chairman of the Federal Reserve. When accepted at Harvard Business School, Chokel repaid his scholarship, which required him to work for a year in journalism. While earning his MBA, he also was editor of *The HarBus News*, HBS' weekly campus newspaper.

After graduation from HBS and two years working in market research, Chokel spent 12 years primarily as a commercial lender for two Cleveland banks. In 1986, he left banking to focus on investing, both as a small time venture capitalist and as an independent investor in the public markets. He provided both funding and advice to more than 40 small private companies over 30 years, primarily in the Cleveland area. His major winner in private investing was Cleveland Vibrator, a manufacturer of industrial vibrating motors and related equipment. He and two others bought the company out of bankruptcy in 1990 and built it to consistent profitability. Jeff was CEO from 1992 to 2007, and remains chairman of this family-owned firm.

Personal interests include tennis and fitness training, especially on a stationary rower. Travel has also been a long-time passion. Between college years, he went to Europe, bought a Lambretta motor scooter in Milan, and drove it 5000 miles one summer. He also hitchhiked throughout Europe with his girlfriend (now his wife of 46 years) after completing his academic education. In the past 15 years, they have visited Argentina, Chile, Hong Kong, Singapore, Bangkok, Phuket, Bali, Australia, New Zealand, Mexico, the Galapagos, Machu Picchu, India, Sri Lanka, and Morocco.

Those wishing to comment on the book or contact the author should e-mail: jdchokel@gmail.com.

ACKNOWLEDGMENTS

THIS BOOK IS DEDICATED TO Pat Chokel, my wife of 46 years and the beautiful blond who drove her Tufts University roommates to an HBS mixer in September of 1968 and stayed to dance with me. She has offered advice in preparing this book in all phases, and has patiently listened to my many and repeated tales of classmates.

I also want to thank my editor, Lisa Bess Kramer at www.clevelandedits.com and her assistant editor, John Deike. They offered much guidance on what to cut and what to expand to make the chapters "sing." Along with proofreader Marsha Goldberg, they also found more mistakes and needed corrections than I dreamed possible. My gratitude also goes to those HBS classmates who took the time to talk with me and share their career experiences and wisdom.

PREFACE

OMPARED TO HARVARD COLLEGE, FOUNDED in 1636 and the oldest institution of higher learning in the United States, Harvard Business School (HBS) is a relative newcomer in the world of education. It was established in 1908 with 15 faculty members, but didn't have its own administration until 1913. Women weren't accepted into the full Master of Business Administration (MBA) program until 1963. HBS's mission now is to "educate leaders who make a difference in the world."

Instruction for those leaders takes place primarily on a well-groomed campus across the Charles River from Harvard College and the other schools connected under the Harvard University banner. The business school sits on a flat piece of land by itself, a castle of capitalism with the river serving as its moat. The half-mile distance from HBS to Harvard College over a bridge is a pleasant walk in spring and fall, but a bitterly-cold challenge in the winter months. The lovely green lawn in front of HBS's Baker Library permits picnics and sit-down discussions when the sun is warm.

In 1968, Harvard's football stadium and other athletic training rooms, along with parking lots, were near the business school. Many Saturday afternoons, fans filled the stadium and cheered for their team while first-year HBS students wrote frantically to finish their WACs (Written Analysis of Cases) that were due down a mail-shoot promptly by 6:00 p.m. on those same Saturdays. Now, the Harvard campus is grandly spreading across the river and offering new educational programs that more tightly close in on, and interact with, the business school. Dorms, recreation facilities, classrooms, and dining facilities have all been significantly upgraded at HBS. Since all students now accepted into the MBA program are expected to have at least a few years of work experience, most anticipate a pleasant and comfortable living and learning environment. The school knows what luxuries must be provided to justify the $72,000 annual tuition and perhaps $150,000 loss of outside earnings during the two-year MBA program.

When the class of 1970 entered HBS, all-in costs for tuition, meals, and housing for nine months were only about $5,000. To me, however, that amount was expensive enough. I relied on my journalism background to help pay my way.

While a student at HBS, I wrote for the campus newspaper, *The HarBus News*. During my second year, I served as its editor, spending 20-plus hours a week for the paper and earning enough to pay for a year at HBS. This work continued an early start writing for my high school newspaper, which resulted in a journalism scholarship to attend Princeton University.

After college, I had a scholarship obligation to go into journalism for a year. Upon acceptance at HBS, however, I repaid the money and sold out to capitalism. I've felt guilty ever since despite being editor of *The HarBus News*. My career has been in banking and investments, surprisingly helped by my journalistic ability to ask pertinent questions. This book is written with the hope of eliminating my remaining guilt, but more importantly, to shine the light on some very talented classmates who have had a wide variety of job and life experiences.

Much of the material for the book has been gathered by interviewing 132 classmates, some in person but most through hour-long telephone conversations. This represents about 20% of the class who are still alive and reachable through school records. All members of the Class of 1970 were invited to participate via an e-mail I sent through the school to the class. About 40% of those I e-mailed directly chose to participate. The interviewing began in the fall of 2010 and has stretched six years. Readers should recognize that while many descriptions are represented as current, they were current as of the date of the interview. For example, a directorship may have been held five years ago, not presently. The index includes all interviewees with respective interview dates.

Those who chose not to participate, I suspect, include some who were not financially successful in their careers and others who were extremely successful but desired privacy.

I usually began our conversation by asking classmates to outline their career progression after graduating from HBS. This often led to comments on experiences that were further explored. Only two specific questions were asked of everyone: (1) How many times have you been married and (2) What is your current wealth? The first question I hoped would indicate family stability. The second was intended to provide an overall indication of financial success, with "wealth" not defined but interpreted by each interviewee. Rather than asking for a specific number, I asked for ranges: under $1 million; $1 – $10 million; $10 – $100 million; and over $100 million. If the results on this question are honest and representative of the whole, joining the Class of 1970 in 1968 was a wise economic decision.

On the question of marriage, 75% of those interviewed reported one and only one marriage. Only three were married more than twice. This matrimonial stability might be because we were smart enough to choose the right partner the first time. Or perhaps we enjoyed enough financial success to avoid the stressful issue of money in a marriage. Perhaps we simply realized how costly a divorce is to both sides. There are certainly other possible explanations as well.

On the financial issue of wealth, 45% of the responding participants said their wealth fell in the $10 – $100 million range, certainly a high enough level to feel quite comfortable. Approximately 43% said they were in the $1 – $10 million range. For the 12% choosing the other two selections (under $1 million and over $100 million), there were more at the higher level than the lower. In fact, only 5% admitted they were not millionaires. My general impression was that the typical interviewee had accumulated around $10 million in wealth. These results might not be representative of the entire Class of 1970 since only about 20% of the class was interviewed, and these people were not randomly chosen.

Each classmate interviewed was given a chance to review what has been written about him or her, both to correct any inaccuracies and soften anything objectionable. My intent was, and is, to be accurate and avoid making enemies. In 2016, most of the 1970 class members still living are in the vicinity of 70 to 80 years of age. Power has peaked, but reflection is coming on strong. This is a good time to ask people to look back.

The Harvard Business School is in no way sponsoring this book. I have had difficulty in confirming what would seem to be simple facts. For example, how many were in the class? Should that number include those entering or those finishing? What should be done with drop-outs, transfers in or out, or those taking a year off? How many students entered straight from college? What number came from outside North America? Simple questions, but the answers either aren't kept by the school or are subject to varying interpretations. In fact, the alumni office of the school declined my request to have someone read this book and offer comments. My impression was that HBS wanted nobody associated with the school to read any alumni book prior to publication, thus avoiding any negative reaction from a graduate on comments made.

INTRODUCTION

O N A LATE SUMMER'S DAY in 1968, some 750 mostly 20-some-things gathered at Baker Fieldhouse next to Harvard's football stadium to be welcomed into the Harvard Business School Class of 1970. Dean George P. Baker glanced at us and said: "Look around you. Never again in your life will you be sitting with such a talented group of people as you are now." He had a smile on his long and distinguished face, perhaps because he anticipated what was ahead for us, or perhaps he knew that he would be retiring in a year after more than three decades on the Harvard faculty.

The words didn't really register with the audience. Looking at my future classmates, they seemed no different than any other group of young people—reasonably well-washed and alert, but with a wide variety of clothes and shapes. There were 29 women and 28 black students, 74 students from outside North America, and about one-third coming straight to graduate school from college. You knew they were special because they were among the one out of four applicants who were accepted that year to HBS. How special and in what ways was to be learned later.

The Class of 1970 was something of an experiment being conducted by a young professor of human behavior named Tony Athos. Professor Athos—tall, thin, and radiating the energy of enthusiasm—had convinced the Admissions Department to let him

1

play a key role in who was accepted in 1968. He wasn't looking for the white male/prep school/Ivy League/great academic types that were common in previous classes. Chosen for the Class of 1970 were football, basketball, and rugby captains, military veterans who were Navy Seals before that name was used, double the number of women of recent years, and more minority students than had been accepted in all previous HBS classes combined. Included among those admitted were the leading salesman for IBM who hadn't even completed college, and a fair number of students who couldn't explain why they were accepted while others worthier on paper were denied. As for me, an OK student with decent (but not the best) business school boards, at college I had written for newspapers as a stringer to earn my spending money. It's likely that not many journalists were applying to HBS in late 1967. I was surprised by my acceptance letter.

Professor Athos was choosing wild cards and hoping we would become productive graduates. In a 1990 article in *Business Week*, Athos was quoted: "We didn't want to admit everyone from Williams and Yale and Harvard, the people who wore wool fabrics and button-down shirts. We looked for people who stirred the pot rather than guarded it. The world was changing, and it was time for Harvard to change."

The world certainly was changing, and the Vietnam War was prompting much of that change. HBS had always supported the efforts of the military, especially during World War II when management programs were devoted to training leaders who could help the war effort. Many servicemen were assigned to these programs. Some thought an important goal of the school was to recruit CIA operatives who could later pursue international business as a cover for agency activities.

By 1968, Vietnam had made life very uncomfortable for male students trying to move on with their lives after college. The draft was taking as many as it could, and the best you could do was guess at your short-term future, not plan it. In Boston, there were frequent protest marches against the war. The term "military-industrial complex" was used as a derogatory phrase for those supporting the war effort. Harvard Business School was identified with this group, presumed to support, or at least tolerate, the war. Some college coeds wouldn't date students who studied there. Harvard College, directly across the Charles River, was a center of protest and enemy territory when viewed from the opposite side. An Air Force pilot on assignment to HBS to get an education threatened to take a jet up and strafe the bridge if protesters crossed the river to trash the HBS campus.

Before graduation in 1970, Harvard College went on strike to protest the war and the Kent State shootings, but the business school continued to hold classes. A vote among black students at HBS was one vote shy of voting to join the educational strike. Some students and professors did hold a week of alternative discussions on the war instead of the regular case studies.

It was not an ideal climate to focus on normal classroom cases and discussions. But for those of us who had been awarded the privilege of earning an MBA from Harvard, we set aside our doubts and moved forward. Though we might have the educational path interrupted by the military or other distractions, we were a determined bunch. What happened after we earned the degree, as we entered the real world, is the subject of this book.

1

CLIMBING THE
CORPORATE LADDER

WHEN THE CLASS OF 1970 entered Harvard Business School in the late summer of 1968, the anticipation was that upon graduation we'd enter the business world as small but potentially important parts of a large corporate machine. We were confident in our ability to rise to the top, or at least near the top, of whatever company we joined. After 20 years of loyal effort and creative contributions, we would become key decision-makers and have the power and prestige to effect change and achieve success. In the process, we'd also become rich.

It didn't work out that way for two primary reasons. First, we learned that moving up the corporate ladder required luck as well as skill. Having the right boss (or bosses), working in the right job at the right time, and even landing in a growing industry that allowed for advancement vs. a corporate culture focused on maintaining the status quo—these were the all-important success factors. Second, there was a shift from two-way loyalty between employer and employee to everyone being responsible for pursuing his or her own best interests. For example, in the mid-'70s, banks in the Cleveland area had an understanding that officers at one bank would not be recruited by another. If an officer left one bank and sought a job at another, the potential new employer would ask permission to hire from the former bank involved. By the mid-'80s, the job scene had transitioned to an "anything goes" job search approach. Employees discovered that loyalty was not rewarded; instead, it was penalized, since new hires often were better compensated than existing employees. A free-for-all of job shifting came as a result.

Those who began a career path that moved steadily forward were as rare as they were lucky. A single corporate employer became very unusual. Even for prestigious HBS graduates, the route to the top began to involve multiple job shifts within a company, and even more frequently shifts that required moving from one company to another. You stayed in one spot only as long as you were learning and appreciated in the job you were doing. When this slowed or stopped, you jumped to another company to move forward.

YOUNGEST CEO EVER

One of the best examples of using various challenges to move ahead was a lanky Mormon basketball player named Nolan Archibald. Very few Class of 1970 grads reached the heights that Nolan did during his career. Nolan had led his Weber State team to the NCAA tournament in 1968 and had earned the status of Academic All-American, one of 15 out of 4,000 basketball players that year to receive the honor. He was accepted at HBS but continued to consider playing professional basketball. In the summer between the first and second year of the MBA program and again right after graduation, he went to the Chicago Bulls rookie camp for basketball tryouts. The second time he went, he was the last person cut from the team. He was, however, unlikely to play with Michael Jordan, who joined the Bulls in 1984.

As he left basketball behind, Nolan thought about his HBS classes where the academic case studies students discussed often ended with a question: "What would you do as CEO and why?" Nolan set his sights on becoming the CEO of a Fortune 500 company. His first job decision was whether to work for a big company (Proctor & Gamble) or a small Texas conglomerate with a variety of business interests. He chose the latter and was sent to Montreal to be acting general manager of a ladies' knitwear company with $3 million in annual sales and $1 million in annual losses. After two months, a president was brought in, but this newcomer quickly left the job when he saw the difficulties he faced. Nolan became general manager, and in two years turned the firm around and sold it.

Nolan's next assignment was with a snowmobile company in Quebec. He became president and moved the marketing and finance parts of the business to Burlington, Vermont. After building sales for four years, he sold it "for a lot" to the Japanese company Kawasaki. He then had other assignments with a boat company and a staff position working on mergers and acquisitions. In each of these varied assignments, he said he didn't care about title or compensation. "I asked whether this would prepare me for a job as CEO of a Fortune 500 company."

The challenges he had successfully dealt with attracted the attention of a larger conglomerate — publicly traded Beatrice Foods. He joined them as VP of marketing for Airstream Trailers and then became president of two turnaround situations: Delmar Window Coverings and Stiffel Lamps. Soon, he was asked to be president of all of Beatrice's $2 billion non-food businesses. His wife commented, "They must be desperate," but he took the job. He might have remained at Beatrice, but he had disagreements with a difficult CEO, and decided to move on.

In 1985, Towson, Maryland-based Black & Decker, which over a five-year period was losing market share and money despite $1.8 billion in revenue, decided it needed a new president. Nolan was one of 47 candidates considered. This group was narrowed to ten who were invited with spouses to have further discussions with the executive recruiter and senior management. After Nolan's visit, Nolan said the executive recruiter advised the company, "Forget Nolan and hire his wife," but Nolan got the job. Six months later, the Board of Directors fired the CEO and gave Nolan that coveted title. At age 42 in 1986, he was the youngest CEO ever of a Fortune 500 company.

Within three years, Black & Decker was hitting record sales and profits. The launch of the Dewalt professional power-tool line was a big winner, growing eventually to $2 billion in sales. Less successful was the acquisition of Emhart, which helped B&D grow to $5 billion in sales but left the company with too big a debt load. When a recession hit, there was too much risk. Nolan said that in hindsight he wouldn't have made that acquisition, but eventually the economy turned and the deal was viewed favorably.

One of the biggest challenges the company faced was competing against the Chinese, especially in kitchen appliances. In 1997–1998, U.S. labor costs, with all benefits included, were $18–$25 per hour. Similar costs in Eastern Europe were $3.25, in Mexico $3, and in China $1.50. Black & Decker underwent a major restructuring and became the low-cost producer internationally. In the later stages of his career, Nolan helped engineer his company's acquisition by Stanley Tool Works, the largest hand-tool company. Black & Decker's strength in the power tool business fit Stanley well, and combined company revenues were over $10 billion annually. After the acquisition was completed in March of 2010, Nolan became executive chairman and earned $64 million in 2011. He was cited by *Business Week* as one of the top six managers in the United States. Board memberships included Lockheed Martin, Huntsman Corporation, and Brunswick Corporation. Prior boards were ITT, Johns Hopkins, and Harvard Business School.

When asked to discuss the qualities needed by a CEO, Nolan mentioned intelligence, competence, and especially high personal integrity. He also urged having a sense of humor and enjoying being with people. "Ninety percent of the ballgame for a CEO is developing a strategic plan, both qualitative and quantitative, and finding the right people for the right jobs," he said. He added that choosing people involved four steps: identifying, recruiting, developing, and retaining them to make the company successful.

Success Through Mergers

Another path to CEO, built on various career experiences and a lot of hard work, was followed by Vince Calarco, a chemical engineering grad from Polytechnic Institute of New York University. Vince's skills allowed him 19 years of success as CEO of Crompton Corporation. During his CEO stint from 1985 to 2004, Crompton grew from $200 million to $4 billion in sales, largely by acquiring other chemical firms.

After college, Vince joined Proctor & Gamble. His three years there were interrupted by the Army, which in 1966 was drafting 79,000 per month and sending many to Vietnam. College ROTC and his chemical engineering degree instead earned him two years at Aberdeen Proving Ground (Maryland), where he worked in a lab doing ballistic missile research. When he finished, he moved on as a student at Harvard Business School in 1968.

NL Industries had employed him during the summer between his first and second years, and upon graduation, offered Vince a chance to work in finance for the group VP of chemical operations. He functioned as the VP's assistant, doing a variety of things, including strategic planning. When NL began restructuring under a new CEO, he got the chance to run various small divisions and gain valuable operational experience.

In 1978, Uniroyal invited him to be a senior manager in chemicals and polymers. The following year, he began five years as President of Uniroyal Chemicals, an $800 million revenue operation.

He earned praise for his planning and development efforts, and in 1985 was again recruited, this time as CEO by Crompton & Knowles, an old-line firm with only $200 million in sales. The decision to leave Uniroyal meant joining a company only one-fourth the size, but the CEO title prompted him to accept.

During the 14 years from 1985 to 1999, the economy was generally on the upswing, and Vince took full advantage. It was a lot of fun, he remembered, as he concentrated on instilling a can-do attitude in his management team and creating a culture of making things happen very quickly. He emphasized problem solving for the customer and giving good service, not just selling a product. He said, "Customers learned to rely on us for help" in Crompton's unglamorous business segments: dyes for fabrics, various chemical fragrances, and extrusions for specialized equipment. An equity analyst who met with Vince early on thought the company had little chance to be a stock market out-performer. That analyst later became a big supporter.

The company hit a home run in 1997 when it bought the former Uniroyal Chemical operation, which Vince had run 12 years earlier, thus adding $1.1 billion in sales. Not quite as successful was the purchase in September of 1999 of Witco Chemical, with $1.5 billion in sales. "The economy started tanking right after the purchase," Vince recalled, "and I learned about the potential downside of using debt leverage." He risked violating bank loan covenants and solved the problem by selling Crompton's silicon business to GE for $1 billion.

Vince retired from Crompton as CEO in 2004, finishing a career where he built a company on the strength of a shared vision and 17 different merger/acquisition transactions. At the time, Crompton was considered one of 100 top-performing companies in the United States. Vince continues to be active in private equity investing and is on several company boards, including Consolidated Edison and Newmont Gold, where he has been the non-executive chairman since 2007.

ONE SMART COOKIE

The climb of male HBS grads to the executive office was not easy, but for women still unwelcomed above the glass ceiling in the '70s, getting there was especially difficult. One woman graduate who joined an investment bank after graduation went to client meetings and, according to her, "people just assumed I was there as a secretary or somebody's mistress." Another woman was performing well at a large corporation until a new boss was brought in to supervise her. She got along fine with her new boss, but his wife felt a competitive threat and insisted that she be fired or transferred. Still another female grad married an older man who retired to paint and took her to a summer artists' colony on a small island a two-hour boat ride off the coast of Maine. The summers were fine, but the island was not the best place to put a Harvard MBA to use. This was especially true since a single bulky cell phone (no landlines) was used by all 30 permanent residents. The '70s were also a time when companies offered little assistance to women blending careers and motherhood. Frequently, a one-or-the-other choice had to be made, and once off the corporate ladder, getting back on successfully was often impossible. There were, however, a few who showed a woman could make it in a man's world.

"She was one smart, sharp cookie," says a classmate of Ellen Marram, a marketing whiz who reshaped the food industry with the introduction in the early '90s of low-fat cookies and other healthier snack foods under the SnackWell's brand for Nabisco.

Ellen entered HBS from Wellesley College as part of the 4% female contingent of the class. She more than held her own during the give-and-take of heated classroom discussions. I personally witnessed a determined and persuasive debater when, as editor of the school newspaper *The HarBus News*, I short-changed her on a payment she was due. She wrote a story for the paper at my request, with payment to be at 15 cents per column inch. She submitted 10 inches, but I had to edit out three inches to fit the space available. I paid her for seven inches. After a 15-minute argument over this

45-cent difference, I surrendered, happy to escape with only a verbal lashing. This is the same woman who later joined the board of *The New York Times*.

Ellen's first job was at Lever Brothers where she became a product manager in the food business. Next, she worked for Johnson & Johnson, primarily on new products, and in 1977, she moved to the grocery division of Standard Brands. She worked there for 16 years, but in 1981, the company merged with Nabisco and in 1985, it became part of RJR Nabisco. This last name became famous worldwide when the company was bought in 1989 as the largest leveraged buyout in history. Ellen, at the time, was running the $3 billion (annual revenue) biscuit business. Her marching orders in the first year after the buyout were clear: double EBITDA (earnings before interest, taxes, depreciation, and amortization) while maintaining market share. She and her team met the objective.

In 1993, Ellen joined the Tropicana Beverage Group (part of Seagrams, Inc.) as president and CEO, but left in 1998 after Pepsi acquired Tropicana from Seagrams. For several years, she was a partner in a private equity firm that invested in small and middle market companies focused on healthy living and aging. Today, she is a director or advisor to a number of private companies, primarily in the food and healthcare areas, and serves on several nonprofit boards. In addition to *The New York Times*, she also sits on the boards of Ford Motor and Eli Lilly, and has served on the boards of Kmart and Cadbury Schweppes.

When she looks back at her almost 30 years with large companies, Ellen stressed the importance of making sure every employee understands how his or her job contributes to the whole of the business, and how he or she will be measured and rewarded. In terms of career progression, she suggests avoiding companies where uncontrollable factors (e.g., age and seniority) are criteria for advancement. As for marketing decisions, they are really a combination of science and art. "It's fine to tap into your own consumer reaction, but don't over-generalize from it," she said. "The marketing mistake made most often is not recognizing that different people buy the same product or service for different reasons. You need to segment the market. You also need to be open-minded to what consumers are telling you. There can be too much talking and not enough listening."

Ellen also urged a thorough understanding of a brand's equity value. Nabisco thought that A-1 Steak Sauce, with people eating more chicken than steak, could grow its business by making a poultry sauce. It didn't work because the A-1 equity brand wasn't linked with sauce—it was linked with red meat.

Nabisco's success with SnackWell's came from recognizing that the growing interest in low-fat foods could be applied to the snacking category. In the first year, SnackWell's grew to a $400 million business. Oreos were always Nabisco's best-selling cookie, but shoppers would follow the Nabisco trucks to supermarkets to buy the latest shipment of fat-free Devil's Food cookies before they sold out. Store managers had such a difficult time keeping them in stock that delivered boxes were often locked in the manager's office and then sold to shoppers who had signed up for them.

About smaller companies, Ellen had these observations: "Successful founders and entrepreneurs have made every decision, both big and small, and believe that every decision they've made is the right one. As their companies get to a certain size, one person making all the decisions is no longer feasible. It's really different when a business is bigger and a leader needs to build a team and manage through people. You can't manage one-on-one in a large company. It's also tough to acknowledge that, in certain areas, experts need to be brought in." Her advice: "Sometimes leading is creating and communicating the vision, inspiring people, and then getting out of the way."

A BANKING SURVIVOR

Very few graduates of HBS's Class of 1970 stayed with one employer throughout their careers. Sam Heffner was one who did, retiring from Citibank in 2001. His long career was more remarkable given the many changes in the banking business, where mergers and re-organizations made employer-employee loyalty in either direction a vanishing attribute.

Sam had come to HBS after serving in Vietnam with Army Intelligence. A "B" student in college and a strong tennis player, he turned a good personal interview into an admission to HBS. "They took some chances," he commented. While at HBS, he enjoyed probability analysis, but believes he should have focused more on human behavior in organizations. "I was naïve about politics in the workplace," he said. "You really have to get along with people."

After his experiences in Vietnam, he and his wife decided to live and work in Asia. He was hired by Citibank, and after three months in New York City, he was moved as a trainee to Manila. He had a good start, and in the mid-'70s was transferred to Hong Kong to work as the chief of staff to a senior Citibanker who was also an HBS grad. Sam was quick to recognize some changes that were needed, and his boss adopted each of his recommendations. Sam later heard that in implementing these changes, his boss gave Sam no credit for them. He also became aware that jokes about his boss were frequently made by others, but only in secret because the boss was described as "vindictive."

Sam and his wife were active members of a church in Hong Kong, and declined an invitation to a work party at the bank on Easter Sunday to address a problem that was important but not urgent. He was also bothered when certain favorites of the boss were pointed to apartments that offered low-rent, long-term leases being vacated by some international staffers, while other staffers were left on their own to deal with an inadequate housing allowance. The budgeting process was handled by requiring very aggressive plans from the boss's subordinates, and then combining these plans with a profit haircut to set an easier target for the boss himself. Sam mentioned that this was unfair. His boss was not pleased.

When it came time for Sam's annual review, he received a raise in salary but was passed over for a promotion that generally was routine unless the officer had underperformed. When Sam asked for a meeting with his boss, a secretary informed him that the boss felt there was nothing to discuss. A long way from home with a growing family to support, Sam faced a very serious but not unusual career problem. He had not played the expected role of "yes man" to that boss and was being punished.

Luckily for Sam, another senior Citibank official in charge of the investment banking group in Hong Kong asked Sam to be his chief of staff, a transfer readily accepted. After a year, he was promoted to CEO of merchant banking subsidiaries in Bangkok and then Manila for what he calls the best five years of his 31-year career at Citibank.

After ten years in Asia, Sam and his wife moved back to the United States. He worked for three years in New York City at headquarters where he said he was "just another guy." He was transferred to Seattle for six years, and then back to New York to work in risk asset review, an internal audit function for reviewing credits. He retired from the bank in 2001, and had the good fortune of selling most of his Citibank shares before the roof fell in beginning in 2008 when the price of Citibank's stock sank rapidly. Many other executives with shares didn't want to sell because they would need to pay capital gains taxes, and have since regretted such decisions. The greedy excesses from trading securities and their by-products did not surprise Sam. He noted that the whole trading culture seemed to require "checking an employee's ethics at the door."

UNCLEAR GLASS

Another long and loyal company man was John Van Zanten III. John interviewed with ten firms as a new graduate and chose

Corning, Inc., better known as Corning Glass Works. He retired from the company in 2002 after 32 years, but he had to be flexible in accepting assignments to stay that long with Corning. In 1970, his first assignment was to work on developing a computer screen. This became obsolete in five months when a competitor introduced a new and better screen. He moved to the consumer division and worked with Pyrex, Corning Ware, and Corelle, initially in market research and later as head of that unit. In the early '70s, the company introduced a drip coffee maker to replace the coffee percolator. The new innovation was not accepted by consumers. Three years later, Mr. Coffee came out with a similar product, which became a huge success. Timing is everything.

Corning spent 10% of revenues on R&D, always looking for the next new thing. One success was the flat glass TV screen, which took over the television market. Another was range-top cookware. In 1985, light-sensitive glass was introduced for eyeglasses, and this idea had good international success even though the initial 60–40% mix of plastic to glass later became 98% plastic. Perhaps the most highly touted product was optical fiber, invented to replace copper wire for connecting to the internet. From 1995 to 2000, fiber optic cable became a huge success. Unfortunately, demand didn't continue to grow at the exponential rates anticipated, and competition and technical advances shrank margins.

Corning's stock, which reached $113 per share in 2000, dropped to $1.10 per share in 2002. Employees were let go as the company shrank from 44,000 to 22,000 people in just two years. The staff reductions, however painful, "saved the company," according to John, who was lucky to sell half his Corning stock before the collapse. His decision to sell was made not because he anticipated what was coming, but simply a rebalancing of his portfolio as it became too concentrated in Corning stock. This experience taught him and the company not to take success for granted and not to concentrate your bets.

16

In considering his big company career, John urged doing a lot of up-front preparation and research for any big project. He advised, "When something important is starting, think first what the objective is, then spend more time planning your actions than actually doing them."

INNER CITY TO CORPORATE BOARDROOM

Bob Ryan, one of a couple dozen black MBA grads in the Class of 1970, had a more diverse corporate experience in preparing for a position as an executive in a large firm. He moved from consulting to banking to the oil business before finishing as chief financial officer for Medtronic, a well-respected medical technology firm.

Bob gives much of the credit to his mom and dad for making it from inner-city Detroit to the leadership elite of business as a board member of six major public companies: United Health, Tampa Electric (TECO), Black & Decker, Citigroup, Hewlett Packard, and General Mills. His dad taught him to be accountable, while his mom drilled him on reading and writing (before kindergarten) and enrolled him in Catholic schools for his early training and in a specialized public school for 9th–12th grades. His father was one of 15 children and his mother was a coal miner's daughter.

Bob was the first in his family to attend college. To limit chances of racism and to challenge himself academically, he chose to pursue the science of engineering at Cornell. He liked business better, but believed it more difficult to find racial neutrality in the world of business. He earned two engineering degrees and was working on a Ph.D. when he decided to apply to business school, but only to Harvard. Once accepted, he did well and received a job offer from McKinsey Consulting to work in New York. For five years, he worked on a variety of projects before joining Citigroup on Chairman Walter Wriston's staff. He spent seven years there, including a stint running the lending department for broadcasting and cable television, where two signatures could commit the bank to lend its legal limit.

In 1984, Bob moved to Houston to be CFO of Union Texas Petroleum, then owned by Allied Corp. Kohlberg, Kravis and Roberts (KKR) soon bought 50% and Bob helped KKR buy the rest by structuring a leveraged buyout. He flew around the world to help sell the deal, and personally participated in the buyout, which happened just before oil dropped $30 to $8 per barrel. Almost half the workforce was laid off in 1986 as the company struggled to survive. Bob faced personal bankruptcy if the company went under.

Either through luck or foresight, Bob was reviewing the company's business interruption insurance at the time and decided it should be doubled given the lack of a financial cushion. He doubled the coverage shortly before a major problem stopped production from a platform drilling rig in the North Sea. The insurance helped the company survive.

Luck again was with him when the company was taken public just before the stock market crash of 1987.

After eight years with Union Texas Petroleum, Bob left to be CFO at Medtronic, a medical technology company with 75% gross profit margins and over 10% of revenues invested into research. Although in charge of finances, he learned about the products by visiting operating rooms more than 100 times with Medtronic-exclusive sales reps who were on call 24 hours a day to assist doctors performing operations. He stayed at Medtronic for 13 years and watched its stock go from $4 to $60 per share, with the company generating $2–$3 billion in annual cash flow.

Looking back on his experiences, Bob offered this career advice: "Enjoy the work you do and focus not on pay but on gaining knowledge." His board experiences have been challenging, but the insights gleaned and the opportunity to learn have made retirement "a lot of fun." He does advise potential directors, however, to talk extensively with the CEO and other members of the board to make sure that there is the highest level of integrity and respect, and a good working relationship between management and the board, before accepting a director's seat.

REAL ESTATE, BASEBALL, & AMBASSADORSHIP

Like many classmates, Craig Stapleton became involved with the real estate business in the early '70s. He joined the National Housing Partnership in Washington, D.C., a nonprofit focused on subsidized housing for the less fortunate. Craig remained when it became part of the Ford Foundation and continued to develop housing in poverty areas. After five years, he started advising Ford on its for-profit real estate investments, then moved to a workout role at a real estate trust. His job was to straighten out its troubled loan portfolio. In 1982, his varied experience earned him the president's title at Marsh and McLennan Real Estate Advisors, where he remained until retiring in 2000

Craig concentrated his corporate career in real estate, but this didn't limit his outside activities. He worked on George H.W. Bush's presidential campaign in 1980 and became friends with the younger George W. Bush. When "W" bought the Texas Rangers in 1989, he was part of the ownership group. After the Rangers were sold, he became a co-owner of the St. Louis Cardinals. He helped in the Bush presidential campaigns of 2000 and 2004, and was appointed ambassador to the Czech Republic in 2001. He had 250 people on his staff and encouraged support for American interests when the United States entered Afghanistan and Iraq after the 9/11 attack in New York in 2001. In 2005, he became ambassador to France with 1,200 people on staff. France wasn't very supportive of United States activities in Iraq, but did cooperate on Syria and Iran.

The ambassadorship positions were most rewarding when Craig felt he had an impact on policy, such as encouraging the Czech Republic to join NATO and the European Union, and later smoothing relations with France over disagreements in handling crises in the Middle East. He noted that when he served, about half the ambassadors were career-oriented foreign service officers, while the rest were political appointees.

Board memberships have included the Peace Corps, Flamel (a French pharmaceutical company), the 9/11 Memorial Commission, Abercrombie & Fitch, and the Center for Economic Research and Graduate Education. "I was lucky with my opportunities," he said, having worked with nonprofits, big business, baseball, and the diplomatic corps.

STAYING AT HARVARD

Paul Upson can say he never left Harvard after receiving his MBA in 1970. Positioning himself by emphasizing finance courses at HBS, Paul was hired to administer a newly created program for the university: a summer session offering management training for college administrators. The program's first class had 40 students. Four years later, it had grown to 120 participants before it was merged into Harvard's School of Education.

Paul then took a job as business manager for the Harvard College Library, initially consisting of six libraries and hundreds of employees. He did this for six years, during which time five more libraries were integrated financially into the Harvard College Library. His primary work was annual budgeting, but he had a broad range of financially related responsibilities.

In 1980, Paul became financial officer for the Harvard Law School, budgeting for more than 50 tenured faculty, 300 employees, and 1,800 students. He also oversaw food services, copy centers, facilities management, and building committees. The budgeting process was intense, with income coming from tuition, endowments, and extensive fundraising efforts. Expenses were tailored to match these sources of income. By the time he retired in 2010, he was supervising a $180 million annual budget as chief financial officer and assistant dean.

Paul remembered the various entities under the Harvard umbrella: "Historically we had a great deal of independence because we had our own development officers and alumni relations offices. Our money was our money." Because the Harvard Law School has a large student body and prosperous alumni, tuition costs were relatively low in comparison to peer institutions. He noted that the law school was always required to pay a fee to the university based on its own budget. Now, however, there is more pressure to share donors with other parts of Harvard University.

Paul still volunteers as treasurer for the Harvard University Retirees Association. He also still interacts with many people from his working life. "I lucked out in finding a career that suited my personality," he admitted. "I felt I didn't work in the real world. There was no sense of business or personal conflicts. There were no games, but employees did need to fit in with the culture to succeed."

Moving On

Russ Allen wanted a different experience before embarking on a marketing career, so he joined the Ford Foundation and spent two years in the Philippines helping establish a program to educate teachers. With this international experience behind him, he moved to Proctor & Gamble, which many consider to be the best place to begin a marketing career. He took the lowest paying job, starting in the packaged soap group. He discovered he loved new product development, and later had an opportunity to move from soap to the health care group. He worked for P&G for eight years, and found "they're very thorough in everything they do" and provide great learning opportunities. P&G does have an "up or out" approach to advancing people, and only one in ten recruits makes it to management.

After eight years Russ moved on, joining Bristol Myers Squibb as a product manager. His first two products were high-fiber cookies and a laxative product. He soon became a group product manager for various over-the-counter items dispensed in a hospital, such as vitamins and nutritional drink supplements. He spent much of his time answering questions for doctors. He turned around the company's pediatric vitamin business and was doing well until his fifth different boss wanted to emphasize sales rather than marketing. After five years, Russ moved on.

He joined Eastman Kodak as a strategic planner for what became Eastman Pharmaceuticals. This was a startup within Kodak, working in new areas of chemistry in a building that had been a monastery. The unit went beyond a research function by acquiring Sterling Drug, growing the combination to a billion-dollar business. It sold products throughout the world with the help of a strategic alliance with Sanofi.

Russ remembered the corporate values set by this new entity: "We are a winning team with mutual respect and candor. We are customer driven. We act responsibly. We have a sense of urgency." With such a favorable corporate culture, he said he "wanted to jump out of bed to go to work." Russ stayed at Kodak for ten years until a new CEO was asked to sell off the Sterling Drug group.

In 1996, Russ joined Ligand Pharmaceuticals, a biological firm working on oncology drugs. He established four joint ventures with large pharma companies over his five years there. Two other similar firms he joined were not as successful, so he decided to retire early. His work experiences prompted him to advise: "Don't have too narrow a focus because you'll probably switch careers. Keep a balance between your career and faith, family and friends."

TWENTY BOSSES
Classmate Joe Settimi considers himself lucky to have had a career with 20 different bosses, with only one of whom he had "no chemistry."

Joe stayed on for a few years, but eventually sought another job. "A different work personality can even make a difference at home," he said. "You want to work at a place where you feel inclined to drive yourself."

Joe started his career with American Standard in a small town in western Ohio. His boss was in New Jersey. He found that being in a staff position in a remote facility was not a good situation, so he left to direct operations for a Michigan manufacturer of RVs, and then joined Scott & Fetzer in 1975, turning around its lighting group before the group was sold. He moved to Milwaukee-based Masco where he spent 23 years, first as group VP for industrial products and then as group president. In 1998, Masco Tech was taken public with $2 billion in revenue. "I was very lucky," he remembered. "Masco had fine people, little political infighting, and few meetings. I never heard a loud voice and I never had a written review." The stock prospered as Masco bought companies from entrepreneurs with 20% operating profit margins and kept the entrepreneurs on for at least three years. "The individuals were vital, not just the operating numbers," Joe said.

CROSSING THE POND

David Challen was another banker who was one of the few who spent almost all his career working with the same employer. After graduating, he worked for two years with the advertising firm J. Walter Thompson, which had sponsored his HBS enrollment. In 1972, however, David joined Schroders, a London-based merchant banking firm as the first MBA degree-holder ever hired. He worked in corporate finance alongside the accountants normally hired by the firm. His target markets were firms doing business in London and English firms doing business outside of Great Britain. Among his successes were saving a British manufacturing company that was being pursued in a hostile takeover by a conglomerate. He also helped the British candy-maker Roundtree to get acquired by Nestle to save it from a hostile takeover.

In 2000, Citigroup bought David's group from Schroders and he became vice chairman of the operation. He served as the independent chairman of Citigroup Europe's Governance Group, which met four times a year to represent regulators seeking to assess the degree of risks the bank was taking. He also served on a government takeover panel to make sure shareholders were fairly treated when a corporate acquisition took place.

David is chairman of the audit committees of two companies in the FTSE 100 list. He credits Margaret Thatcher with opening up British financial markets when she privatized both the water and waste disposal industries in the late '80s. "There was a lot of doubt that this was a good idea, but the shares created went up a lot," David said.

SAME, SAME, BUT DIFFERENT

It's not easy to climb the corporate ladder. It's even more difficult when somebody keeps moving the ladder, which happened in the financial industry consolidation during the '70s, '80s, and '90s. Walt Pressey worked for four different firms in his first 25 years out of HBS without ever leaving his initial employer. Walt wanted to be a security analyst, but the president of the Boston Safe Deposit and Trust Co. convinced him instead to work in budgeting and strategic planning. After three years, he became controller and then CFO of the firm's holding company. In 1981, Shearson bought Boston Safe, and then Shearson combined with American Express.

By charging only a $1 fee for a bank-issued certificate of deposit and using these funds to build a portfolio of large variable rate mortgages, American Express saw its banking unit grow its balance sheet from $900 million in 1982 to $16 billion in 1987. It became the fifth largest mortgage originator in the United States. Walt was the chief planning officer and then head of the cash management division. After this large growth, American Express sold most of its banking operation to Mellon Bank. Walt was now part of his fourth organization. He left in 1995 and joined Boston Bank &

Trust, first as CFO and then as president of the holding company before retiring in 2010. During his 15 years with Boston Bank & Trust, employees went from 69 to 850 and assets under management from $350 million to $20 billion.

Walt looked back on his career and offered three observations. First, most people dealing with a problem identify it incorrectly. If you can agree on how to redefine the problem, you can reach agreement on a solution much more easily. Second, when doing mergers and acquisitions, too much emphasis is put on the math. "You first have to look at the people in deciding whether to proceed," he said. Finally, he thinks most schools do a terrible job when explaining the best way to find a job. "Plan on spending much more of your career doing networking," he advised.

BANKING ON CHANGE

Like several other members of the Class of 1970, Forrest Tefft wasn't sure if he'd be able to attend HBS in the fall of 1968. Graduate school deferments for the draft had been suspended except for doctors willing to go into military service after completing their degree. Forrest had been accepted to attend officer training for the U.S. Navy, but began the two-year program at HBS while exploring the possibility of finishing HBS before serving. Four months after starting as a student, he received an order to report to Fort Dix in New Jersey by his draft board. He was scheduled to join the Army. He contacted the Navy and they agreed to let him finish his school year before going to officer training. This he did, working for the Navy's Supply Corps in Washington, D.C., for two years after Officer Candidate School. It was a good learning experience, Forrest said, and he returned to Harvard and finished his MBA in June, 1973. He chose to remain with the HBS Class of 1970, where he had been with the same 90 classmates for all his first-year classes, rather than be listed with the Class of 1973.

In 1973, Forrest began a 35-year career in banking with six different banks, interrupted only by four years with two private firms. His only regret was not starting in New York City, where, according to him, it's easier to make your financial mark and be a major player in the area of corporate finance. Instead of New York, Forrest returned to Ohio, where he and his wife were raised. He first joined Union Commerce Bank in Cleveland, then an aggressive bank run by two ex-Citicorp execs. But Union Commerce's lending portfolio, especially in real estate, was having trouble in a tough economy and soon had major difficulties, forcing retrenchment and eventual sale.

National City Bank, also in Cleveland, hired Forrest as a commercial lender and soon shipped him to London for the prestigious assignment of running its office there. It was a great opportunity for a young banker, and for three years he took full advantage. He discovered, however, that the office was a profit loser, so he spent his time cultivating English companies that had subsidiaries and banking needs in Ohio, and Ohio companies that could use financial help in Europe. The office became profitable. When the bank's CEO came for a visit, Forrest showed him around in fine style and earned the joking comment: "Dammit, Forrest, I thought I had the best job at the bank!"

Upon returning to the United States, Forrest was recruited to join Mellon Bank in Pittsburgh as manager of its multinational lending group. He later started a leveraged finance group that helped large firms arrange acquisitions, private placements, loan syndications, and equity investments while providing merger and acquisition advice. As manager of corporate finance, he had a staff of 35 and was generating annual fees for the bank in the $25 million range.

After 15 years at Mellon, Forrest said he hit a roadblock when someone who viewed him as a competitor within the bank started a campaign to discredit him. Forrest could have waged war but instead decided not to compromise his principles in a dirty fight and chose to look for a new job. Similar nastiness was encountered in two other positions during his career, and he said this becomes more common as an individual moves up the corporate ladder. "Sometimes you meet people who would throw a member of their own family out of a moving vehicle to get ahead," he said. Each individual has to decide his or her own response to such a challenge when climbing the corporate ladder.

Forrest moved on to Huntington Bank in Columbus, then to First Commonwealth Bank in Pittsburgh, and later Citibank in Pittsburgh. When Citibank decided to close its Pittsburgh operation, he was asked to move to Philadelphia, but a working wife in Pittsburgh and proximity to his daughter and her family in Columbus prompted him to decline. "I loved what I did," he said, especially in working as "agent banker" where you help a client arrange a financing deal with a group of banks. "You're like a chef, creating a meal for 30 people (the other bankers and client) who all have to agree it's good," he said. He's particularly proud that he has never been agent in a deal where the bank lost $1 of principal.

Forrest noted that the changes in banking continue. At Citibank, for example, there are 270,000 employees worldwide, and the bank is looking to hire 13,000 more to add to the 9,700 "compliance people" it now employs to respond to governmental regulations and monitoring. "This means that 8% of the bank's workforce will not be working on profit generation," but will instead be trying to comply with regulations. He also looks back on his career not sorry that he made sacrifices to assure that the interests of his wife and child were not overlooked during his job shifts. "It just felt right," he said.

NEVER COMPROMISE YOUR ETHICS

One of many classmates who found success in the real estate arena was Jim Hambright. While at school, he became interested in government-sponsored housing, which at the time allowed developers to borrow 90–100% of the funds needed for a project. He joined the Phillips Group and helped build 3,500 housing units in the southeast United States. Most were sold through limited partnerships, which allowed investors large write-offs in the early years because of the leverage. Those living in the units, however, often had financial problems, which caused losses for the owners. Jim concluded, "Nobody should ever invest in a deal just because of the tax benefits." Jim hired some social workers to help the renters and moved on to Atlanta.

In Atlanta, he initially worked for a firm doing both development and real estate management. After 2½ years, he joined Crow Carter & Associates as head of its commercial management division, remaining five years. Next, was a challenging position with Adams-Cates & Company; developing a major commercial property complex. Jim headed marketing and also handled managing the offices. He discovered that many properties with institutional investors were poorly managed, a problem he solved "with a detailed approach to everything and zero-based budgeting."

In 1980, Jim moved to Houston to be president of a real estate asset management company handling offices and industrial buildings. In 1985, he returned to Atlanta to set up his own firm as a real estate broker and consultant. He handled all income properties including office, retail, and apartments. He got married in 2005 and began reducing his working hours.

Jim regrets not keeping in better touch with his classmates while he was building his career. Better contacts would have helped him, he said. He warned those who pursued real estate to "never compromise your ethics," and to "make sure you put the client's interest first and to be frankly honest." He remembers that in the early '70s, Atlanta banks and REITs (real estate investment trusts) would give anybody money. He observed, "Being on the conservative side is never a bad thing for a developer."

Sell at the Top

Another classmate who made his mark in real estate was Rob Perrielo, a college engineering grad who was in the Army and worked as

28

a consulting engineer before entering HBS. "I wanted to change career paths," he explained. During his summer break at HBS, he worked for Beacon Construction and joined the firm full-time after graduation. He focused on office buildings prior to becoming CFO in 1977. In 1994, this REIT went public as Beacon Properties. Soon after, $1 billion was raised to do further property investing, and in 3½ years the stock moved from $17 to $43 per share. In mid-1997, concern about the real estate outlook prompted the company's sale to well-known real estate developer Sam Zell in a stock-for-stock deal. Rob sold his new stock immediately and then watched as real estate crashed. He spent the next seven years traveling, handling his own investments, and doing some real estate consulting.

His advice to those entering his profession is to learn "to deal with people and appreciate them—this is very important." He also warned that politics in the office can often outweigh rational decisions, so don't be surprised by what happens. If the real estate market shows weakness, "lease properties at whatever price you can get." Finally, you have to find a way to balance family and career. "I didn't do that well," he admitted with regret.

DEVELOPING AN AUDIT EXPERTISE

Like several other of his classmates, Bill Reardon left after his first HBS year to fulfill his military obligation, in his case, three years as a Supply Corps officer for the United States Navy. He finished his second year at HBS in 1973 and joined the accounting firm Coopers & Lybrand in Boston. He didn't join the family business as he expected because an aptitude test he took showed him as unlikely to succeed in sales. There were seven HBS grads with the Boston office, three of whom later made partner, including Bill in 1980. His audit work was primarily for utilities and nonprofits, but later he developed expertise in the biotechnology area. He retired in 2002 and was on the boards of three public life science companies.

Bill said that accountants, as ordered by the SEC, now have to leave an account at least every five years to provide a fresh look at a company's financials. He's not in favor of this mandated rotation, noting that even a new auditor will not find fraud if it's carefully crafted in the financials. He enjoyed his career work, and encourages people to "try to determine what matters to you." In his case, family and music were very important, the latter maintaining a skill he learned as leader of the Harvard Glee Club as an undergraduate. He also urged people to take jobs that allow "working with people who are interesting, smart, and have high integrity."

BE READY FOR CHANGE

"Don't expect to work for just one company." This advice came from Tod Hamachek for those looking to pursue a business career. "A career is like a tape measure," he said. "You pull it out to all 36 inches, but then it shrinks fast. I worked for five companies and never thought I'd switch around. There's just so much change."

Tod started out at the Harris Corporation, working in the web press division. When a 40-week strike challenged the company's operations, the CEO suggested Tod move into sales, which he did for five years, becoming national sales manager for newspaper presses. Since Harris by then was moving more into electronics, he decided to leave and join his family's company in the brewery industry. This was subsequently sold to a larger company, which then started breaking up its new acquisition. He moved on in 1984 to the Penford Corporation, which had specialty paper, food starches, and pharmaceutical divisions.

Tod prospered and became first Penford's president and then CEO. In 1997, the pharmaceutical arm required more attention to achieve its potential, so Tod spun it out as an independent firm and became chairman and CEO of Penwest Pharmaceuticals. During the next eight years, the company promoted its particular expertise in pharmaceutical powders and delivery systems, including the timed-release capsule. The company's customers included virtually every pharmaceutical firm in North America and Europe. The emphasis was put on powders, including the reformulation of existing drugs, since 75% of the top 100 drugs sold in the United States are delivered orally to the patient. Tod retired in 2005 and Penwest was sold in 2010.

Numerous directorships keep Tod busy, including Northwest Natural Gas Company, where he has been a director since 1986 and chairman since 2012. Among other directorships are the DeKalb Genetics Corporation, the *Seattle Times*, the Sun Valley Center for the Arts, and the Virginia Mason Medical Center, which he described as being the lowest cost and highest quality health provider in the Seattle area.

FINDING A BUSINESS THROUGH PROBLEM SOLVING

Like Forrest Tefft, Ken Frederick had a military responsibility to serve in the Navy, which would allow him only one year of business school before he had to attend Officer Candidate School. He had been accepted by both Harvard Law and Harvard Business schools, and thought interrupting the two-year business program would be easier than suspending the three-year law program. He joined the Class of 1970 at HBS, served three years in the Naval Supply Corps, and then came back for a year to finish his MBA.

Upon graduation he joined Raychem, then a $40 million revenue firm based in San Francisco that was developing specialty materials and plastics. Ken remained with Raychem for 26 years, changing jobs on average every two years, often with a different location as well as function. He was assigned target accounts, but it was up to him to figure out how to sell them something. "We took things to the customers and got them to tell us what they needed," he said. At times he tried to get new technology introduced to the Navy, and he also worked in Europe and Asia. The combined emphasis on sales and R&D paid off for Raychem, which grew sales to $2.4 billion by 1999, when Tyco bought the company. He explained, "You have to figure out the trends and work on them. It's problem-solving to create business. It's all about the customer."

After the Tyco purchase, Ken left and worked at a new software company and then a couple other startups. In 2005, he went on the board of Molecular Imaging Corporation as a director. At his first meeting, the company's auditors resigned and would not provide a "going concern" opinion. The company was leasing equipment to do PET scans for cancer at both fixed sites and elsewhere using mobile trucks. It suffered when fees for the service dropped from $2,600 to $800 per image as Medicare cut back on its payments. The company went into bankruptcy and Ken spent 1½ years trying to settle creditor claims. Ken warned that small companies are vulnerable, especially when dependent on a single large customer. "I'm a big fan of bankruptcy now," he admitted.

A LIFESTYLE DECISION

Peoples Heritage Bank was George Bruns's first employer, but bank mergers and acquisitions resulted in his working there—and eventually for the First National Bank of Boston—for 29 continuous years. For 14 years, he worked in commercial lending to large companies. Industries included high tech, agriculture, and motion pictures, with the latter allowing him twice to attend the Academy Award ceremonies. While lending was fun and glamorous, George made what he called "a lifestyle decision" to switch to the credit review side of banking. "After 10 to 15 years of banking, I let my family take priority," he said. "I didn't want to travel with small children at home."

In 1984, he started running a professional education program within the bank to improve credit skills. When the First National Bank of Boston merged with Fleet Bank and was then acquired by

Bank of America, George decided it was time to leave. He joined the Toronto Dominion Bank as head of credit policy and administration. He remained there for 8½ years before retiring and joining the faculty at the Risk Management Association, a banking trade organization in Philadelphia.

He now is very comfortable and only teaches 20 days a year. "People should understand that money isn't everything," he said. He warned investors to watch out for any banker who says he's going to be the biggest and the best. "Senior managers tend to want to protect their positions, so they want to increase earnings quarterly. Even after the time is passed to do certain things, goals are set high. That's when crazy things are done to increase earnings."

SMALL TO BIG, BIG TO SMALL

Most entrepreneurial startups go nowhere, and the first two John Brown was involved in fit that category. As a first-year student, he and a classmate tried making a rock video, but it failed. A second-year business, started with several classmates to sell posters, paper lamps, fringe vests, and artificial flowers, did better. John stayed with it for a year after graduation, but eventually realized that also wasn't likely to be a big winner. John took a job with a small specialty chemical company in 1971.

This company was sold in 1977 to the Swiss giant Ciba-Geigy, and John ran that company's North American specialty chemical operations after the purchase. In 1984, he spent three months learning German and moved to Switzerland to become head of worldwide marketing for specialty chemicals. In 1988, he became a senior VP, transferred to the pharmaceutical side of Ciba-Geigy, and moved back to the United States to search for promising investments in healthcare. He did this for ten years.

After more than 20 years with Ciba, he entered a ten-year entrepreneurial period where he ran a physician management company and was CEO of a biopharma manufacturing company, and later a firm making equipment for that industry. These latter two were sold and in 2008, and he joined Bausch & Lomb as president of its London-based unit responsible for Europe, the Mideast, and Africa. He retired two years later and moved to Napa Valley in California.

Looking back, John said he would have made a lot more money if he had gone to Wall Street to work after graduation. Nevertheless, he's happy with his choices. "I tried to make the most of the opportunities that presented themselves," he said. "I worked with large and small companies, and enjoyed the exposure to different industries and international business. I broadened my horizons and had good learning experiences." His advice for others: "Get out of your comfort zone, both in business and your personal life."

A WEST COAST GUY

Life style choices were also important for Bob George, who declined to return to his summer banker's job in New York City after graduation. "I'm a West Coast guy," he explained, choosing to work instead in San Jose, California, with the large conglomerate FMC. He spent two years as an internal auditor, traveling for three weeks at a time to various FMC units to review their accounting. "I learned about a lot of different businesses," he said, but he left the company when FMC moved to Chicago.

In 1972, he moved to Portland, Oregon, to join GATX in their business of equipment leasing. He spent 17 years with GATX, first in Los Angeles, then Singapore, Houston, and finally San Francisco. In the latter years, he specialized in aircraft leasing, calling on airlines around the United States. He developed an expertise that was helpful, but found that banks had a lower cost of funds and so were challenging competitors. He solved the problem by joint-venturing with insurance companies, thus lowering funding costs.

He was doing well until 9/11 of 2001, when air travel dropped precipitously due to the terrorist attack on the World Trade Center in New York. The market for new planes was dead for two years. Bob said leasing aircraft "wasn't fun anymore," so he retired at age 55.

Bob's advice to those pursuing business careers is "look at the big picture." He estimated that 75% of all corporate acquisitions are deemed to be failures within three years. You have to review such situations "from up high," and not be weighed down with details. The value of HBS, in his opinion, was not the studies but being forced to make weighty decisions with imperfect information. "You have to focus on what's important, and surround yourself with good people so you can all rise together."

FLYING HIGH

Early on, classmates knew that John Anderson was going to be a "high flier," easy to say since he had been an active airline pilot before coming to HBS, using his undergraduate degree in forest management to look at stands of timber from the air. Upon graduation, he moved to Jacksonville, Florida, to join South Pines, a forest products company. He stayed on when it was bought by St. Regis and he became general manager of the timber and lumber division. He left when St. Regis was bought by Champion. He joined Patriot Transportation Holding, a company developing land from Florida to Washington, D.C. Patriot also had a trucking division. He remained for 19 years, becoming president and CEO.

John viewed his business life as divided into two different careers linked by his "generalist" approach to management. "You've got to like people to be a leader," he said. "Help people feel good about themselves and they will do their best work. People are the most important asset, and they never appear on the balance sheet." He said our culture has drifted off the center line when it comes to personal values. He observed, "Talent and integrity are not necessarily the same. We need to reward those doing what's best for the group versus adopting an approach of recognizing those who make decisions based on what's best for only them."

John witnessed two bad embezzlement situations, first with a business partner and then with a country club that lost $1 million. He urged business people to be particularly alert in the area of nonprofit management. People assume integrity in volunteer activities. A policy of "trust but verify," however, should also be applied to nonprofits.

CFO for General Motors

The path to becoming chief financial officer for General Motors was long and winding for classmate Mike Losh, requiring numerous relocations. When Mike graduated from a Dayton, Ohio, high school in 1964, he furthered his education by going to GM's engineering school in Flint, Michigan. This work-study co-op program, now known as Kettering University, was a four-year program that prepared students for employment at GM. Those fortunate enough to finish in the top 10% of their class were rewarded with further study towards a master's degree, not necessarily in engineering. Mike applied for and was accepted at Harvard Business School, with expenses fully paid by GM.

Mike returned to GM with an MBA in hand and spent his first two years working in a Dayton division that made car parts. From there he was moved to the treasury staff at GM in New York City. "It was a wonderful place for a young person to get a good overview of a major corporation," he said. "At the time, the office was also the greatest developer of financial talent in the world." Mike stayed four years before being sent to Detroit to work on setting product and financial strategy for the company.

After three more years, he was sent in 1979 to Brazil, arriving when inflation was climbing 6% a month and the economy was out of control. Mike found the experience fascinating and a great development experience. Major devaluations of the currency and capital controls caused the country's "lost decade" (the '80s) despite Brazil's high potential. The work force dealt with the problems caused by the government with speed of action and flexibility, cashing pay-checks as quickly as received. The economy was in shambles but "we had an export orientation that allowed us to prosper," he said. One example of the "make it happen" approach was when GM closed its operations in Argentina and wanted to move the massive automotive stamping presses to Brazil. A large barge was chartered and the presses moved north and then were hauled overland to Sao Paulo. While the plant was being completed, the presses were placed on temporary pylons and put into use immediately.

The next assignment, as head of operations in Mexico, came in 1982 just as the Mexican government announced a major devalua-tion and took all bank accounts based in dollars and converted them to pesos at a below-market rate. This effectively devalued the worth of bank accounts. Mexico also nationalized its private banks, allow-ing only Citibank to operate normally in part because it had been doing business in the country since the oil industry nationalization in the '30s. These actions hurt businessmen but, as Mike remem-bers, "it was again a wonderful time to be an exporter, which GM de Mexico was."

In 1984, Mike returned to the U.S. and became general man-ager of GM's Pontiac division. Although manufacturing the cars was handled as a separate unit, Mike had sales responsibility for several thousand employees and 3,000 dealers. He helped grow Pontiac to be the 3rd largest passenger car supplier in the industry with 600–800 thousand cars sold per year. His reward for succeeding was being asked to turn around the Oldsmobile brand, which he did for three years before becoming group VP of all car and truck divisions. His focus was on sales, marketing and service, with seven of his former peers reporting to him. His main challenge was working to reduce competition and build cooperation among the various divisions.

After 12 years in various automotive operating positions, Mike returned to the financial side in 1994 when he became CFO of

General Motors. He was responsible for the $200 billion in auto loans (with the GMAC unit) and $100 billion in pension assets, as well as accounting and the financial health of the company as a whole. Over 10,000 employees supported these efforts. He was based in Michigan but spent time in New York City every other week. Mike is very proud that GM continued as a training ground for financial expertise and future CFOs of other companies. His 36 years with GM came to an end in 2000 when differences with then-chairman John Smale and family issues helped him decide it was time to retire.

Mike's financial experience has been well-utilized in Board of Directors positions in eight major companies and a startup. One of these was Cardinal Health, which he joined in 1996 after he encountered HBS classmate and Cardinal founder Bob Walter while on a Utah horse trail ride with his family. Not only did Mike become a director, but he also served as interim CFO in 2004 for almost a year when an SEC investigation prompted the departure of the former CFO. Cardinal was founded in 1971 as a food wholesaler. In 1979, the company became a drug wholesaler with an acquisition that later moved it to the 26th largest company in revenue on the Fortune 500 list and a $25 billion market-cap now. Other current board positions include Masco, where he serves as chairman of this 32,000-employee building materials company; AON, a $25 billion market-cap British insurance company; H.B. Fuller, a specialty chemical company working with adhesives; and Prologis, a $22 billion market-cap REIT with over 600 million square feet of properties across the globe.

When asked about serving on such major boards, Mike advised people to "understand what you're getting into, and be prepared to step up if called upon." He cited his experience at Cardinal Health, where he stepped into the CFO role. "When a problem arises, sometimes there's nobody to deal with it except you." As for making progress up the corporate ladder of a big company, he suggested it helps to "love the industry, the products, and the people." He added that "every three or four years you should ask the hard question about whether or not you are happy with what you are doing, and what the future looks like."

From Poverty to Portraits

Growing up in the Watts section of Los Angeles in the '50s was not the best place to initiate a business career. Len Fuller didn't let that slow him down. His mother was a seamstress, but her work ethic and the efforts put forth by BBQ-joint owners and other store-front proprietors provided plenty of role models. "I had black heroes who were in business from the time I was a child," Len remembered.

When he finished HBS, a professor suggested he sign on with Crossroads Africa to go to Kenya as group leader, at age 23, of 26 people who spent the summer building an elementary school in Nairobi. The experience led to 20 subsequent trips to Africa and a job offer 13 years later to be executive director of Crossroads Africa. At the time, he was working for Coopers and Lybrand (now Price Waterhouse Coopers) in Detroit as a consultant and turned down the opportunity.

After the initial summer working in Africa, Len became the first black professor in the business school at California Polytechnic University, where he taught for two years. He left to take a job at Douglas Aircraft as a researcher for worldwide aviation. From there, he joined Hughes Helicopters and spent three years in executive positions with the marketing division. This work included being named international marketing manager for Africa, where he oversaw the firm's efforts in 46 countries. After that, he went to Washington, D.C., to help run a 40-person consulting operation.

In 1982, he joined Coopers and Lybrand and in three years became a partner. Of the firm's 1,300 total partners, at the time fewer than ten were black. His work was acting as a consultant in finance, planning and local government, especially for the city of Detroit. In the early '80s, the U.S. State Department hired Coopers & Lybrand to start business training programs for black people in South Africa. This was before Nelson Mandela left prison to run the country. Len led this consulting assignment for Coopers. He found it difficult to find a place suitable to live for his wife and three-year-old son and decided to return to Detroit. Although he enjoyed both Coopers and the work, he and his wife were anxious to return to southern California. In 1990, he moved to Los Angeles to start his own consulting firm from scratch.

"I took a lot of risks in my business life," Len said. When he moved to Los Angeles he mitigated the risk of starting his own consulting business by keeping an office in Detroit. In 1992, he made 40 round-trips from southern California to Detroit to do consulting work in both places. Now his work is primarily done out West. He does still travel a lot, since he sits on 14 mutual fund boards, including the Investment Company of America, the oldest and largest fund in the American Funds family.

Working with mutual funds "keeps me excited," Len said. He observed that "there are a lot of smart people on these mutual fund boards and nobody dominates the discussions," which include the fund's results, the audit report, governance, and the outlook for the economy. He does, however, have to read 1,000 to 2,000 pages in preparation for each meeting. This work keeps him busy now. In between board meetings, he pursues his hobby as an amateur artist, and is credited with painting 90 portraits over the past ten years.

RIGHT ON TARGET

Becoming president of the upscale discount chain named Target involved a long corporate climb through a changing retail environment for classmate Ken Woodrow. Ken's first job after college was working in New York for Bankers Trust and included an assignment in the bank's London office. This experience convinced him of the importance of experiencing other cultures in pursuing a career. After graduating from HBS, he started a consulting firm with three other grads. Their first client was Dayton-Hudson Corporation (DHC), formed through the merger of Dayton's and Hudson's department stores. In 1962, DHC had started Target, believing the proliferation of low margin retailers was a threat to higher margin classic department stores. From its earliest days, Target conveyed an upscale image to customers. It was this image that Target would hone for the next 40 years as the key to differentiating itself from competitors in the marketplace.

Ken's career as a consultant lasted less than one year since he quickly joined Target as a full-time employee. He discovered that discount retailing was in its infancy but growing fast. "Initially our strategy was simple: put up as many stores as we could as fast as we could," he said. "There was lots of room in the market for everyone in the early days." By the early '80s, competition had become intense. Discounters began to disappear due to mergers, acquisitions, and a failure to carve out a sustainable position in the marketplace. Unlike its competitors Walmart and Kmart, Ken said Target continued to reinforce its appeal as a discounter offering fashion and attractive brands at a compelling price, backed by friendly service and an appealing, uncluttered store format.

During Ken's first 24 years at Target, he held a wide variety of management positions: financial analyst, marketing and stores' controller, assistant to the company's chairman, managing a store for two years, serving as a divisional merchandise manager, heading up the distribution function, and serving as chief financial officer. Ken observed, "I was always a big believer in getting to know the key functions of an organization as opposed to focusing exclusively on vertical movement. Early-on horizontal career movement was great in developing management skills, appreciating the importance of teamwork, and gaining an overall perspective on the business."

Also during these years, Dayton-Hudson streamlined its operations, selling its real estate division along with B. Dalton Bookstores and a chain of high-end jewelry stores, and ultimately the department stores as well. After the sale of its Marshall Field's unit, the parent adopted Target as its corporate name and retained its Minneapolis headquarters.

Ken said, "This was most gratifying after the consistent effort and hard work so many had expended to make Target a household name."

When Ken was named president of Target in 1994, he had seen the company grow from 17 stores when he started to about 800 stores, all in the United States. During that period, while management was busy dealing with its primary competitor (Walmart), newer entrants arrived such as category killer Toys-R-Us and later internet marketers like Amazon. Target responded by deepening its expertise in sourcing and brand management. It also brought a unique emphasis on design to its merchandise offering, and introduced a host of captive brands, all designed to reinforce the idea of what Ken said was "great fashion at an unbeatable price." It took advantage of a centrally-based replenishment system, which allowed company buyers to monitor which products were selling in real time and adjust inventory as needed. Target didn't create but benefited from its customers' adoption of the French pronunciation "Tarzhay" to characterize the upscale image of the stores and product offerings. Ken continued as president until 1999 and then finished his 30 years of service (in year 2000) as vice chairman of the company.

In looking back, Ken said he was lucky to remain based in the Minneapolis area for his entire career, although he did travel frequently. He admitted that today it's more of a challenge to spend your entire career with just one company, especially with global competition coming into the United States market. He observed: "Younger people can be unrealistic in what they want and how fast they want it. You have to be a producer, to develop skills, and learn how to manage in a team-building environment." He suggested if a person is highly entrepreneurial, "he should get his feet wet with a startup and see how he likes it." If a person wants to prosper in a big company, "get experience as widely-based as possible."

Since retirement, Ken has served on a variety of corporate boards, including Duane Reade (New York drug stores), Visteon (a conglomeration of businesses divested by Ford), Shock Doctor (protective wear for sports), and Hamline University (St. Paul, Minnesota). Currently, he is a director of Delta Airlines, where he has served for 12 years.

2

How Not to Fall
from the Ladder

FOR THOSE PURSUING LONG-TERM SUCCESS in a corporation, having luck on your side can be a major advantage. Your company may get bought out, an encouraging boss may be moved elsewhere, and corporate strategy may shift in a direction not to your liking. All of these situations may impede your progress, as might your health, family situation, a wrong decision, and countless other factors. Relying on luck, however, is not as helpful as carefully thinking ahead about the challenges you are likely to face.

Before accepting a job, consider whether an industry is moving forward or falling behind. Joining an American coal company in 2010 would probably have limited a person's progress regardless of individual capabilities. In a similar fashion, does your particular company resemble a setting sun or a rising sun? Is upward progress sustainable? Can you contribute in a meaningful way? On the personal side, will a longer-term commitment require relocation, perhaps internationally? How will your family, present or future, deal with job moves? Often, after a dozen years of advancement, personal factors sap one's limitless loyalty to a company and prompt consideration of other opportunities. Many younger people are happy to take a seemingly good job without properly thinking where it might lead and at what costs.

Another factor to consider is corporate culture and your ability to adapt to it. Does advancement come to people who add ideas or mostly depend on age and seniority? Are you a person who wants to work with people who are interesting, smart, and have high integrity? Better choose wisely. Will your personal ethics be compromised by what you might be expected to do? In the banking industry, there have often been instances where lending people have been expected to build loan volume without consideration of what might happen to the borrower, and ultimately, to the bank. Are you willing to say "no" to your boss and risk your job to do the right thing as you view it? You'll want to limit confronting such situations by choosing a company carefully.

Once you've accepted a job, go to where the challenges are even if this sacrifices prestige and compensation. Companies want managers who can solve problems and aren't afraid of tackling challenging assignments. You might fail, but if you gain respect for your effort and intelligence in dealing with it, you'll get another opportunity to prove yourself. Lying low and hoping you won't be noticed is a quick way to get added to the inevitable lay-off list when corporate belt-tightening occurs. Never assume a large company believes you're irreplaceable. The U.S. Army and firms like Proctor & Gamble know that the higher the level you reach, the more difficult it is to move upward in a narrowing climb to the top. When you plateau, you're expected to exit. This is not cruel when it pushes you to another job situation where you'll have an opportunity to progress rather than stagnate. In fact, setting a similar policy for yourself may be something you'll want to adopt regardless of what organization you're in.

While a good product is important, the most critical thing a company has is good people. They don't appear on the balance sheet, but they'll allow a company to deal with surprises that occur for all businesses. An intelligent manager has to learn to appreciate people, and offer encouragement. As one interviewee said, "You've got to like people to be a leader." The best manager isn't necessarily the star, but the person who can motivate others around him to be stars. You manage through people, not with personal dominance. Sometimes people competing for higher slots will do nasty things to move up. Such internal politics are a fact of corporate life, but nastiness can come back to haunt you. When executive recruiters obtain references for candidates being considered for top-level jobs, they'll contact not only previous bosses, but also a person's peers and people who were reporting to the candidate to get a full picture of performance. Many managers who appear good to their bosses show another side to those below them. Criticizing your boss, your peers, or your subordinates will not reflect well on you. If suggestions for improvement need to be made, do it privately.

Even the best managers cannot control their individual destiny, so don't focus too narrowly since you'll probably have to switch companies and maybe careers. A wide base offers better stability as you move up. Try to build experience in all key functions of an organization so you have familiarity with the whole rather than a concentrated knowledge of a small part of the entity. Stop and review your progress every three or four years and consider where it's leading you. Also review the balance you have between career and family so your work isn't causing friction on the home front. If you become dissatisfied with where you are, look for another position elsewhere but be careful about letting that information be known. Some companies follow a policy of terminating immediately an employee who is looking for another job.

Assuming you reach the upper echelons of a company, your main responsibility is to be aware of the big picture. Are your margins and market share going up or down? What threats and/or opportunities do you see? At HBS, one of the first questions students are asked to consider in many cases is, "What business are you in?" For example, do you think in terms of the phone industry or the communications industry, or perhaps the car business or the transportation business? Another way of asking the question is, how much turf are you able to claim, and can you defend it and avoid dilution if you go after too much? One way to expand quickly is to make acquisitions, but if the culture and strategic fit aren't right, problems occur. Many financial experts believe that 75% of all acquisitions are deemed to be failures after three years. It's also dangerous to rely on government support, which could be withdrawn, or a few large customers to make your operations a success.

One of the biggest set-backs to you personally can happen if you stay with a firm for a long period of time and have accumulated company stock and options, 401k plans (holding company stock), retirement benefits, and a comfortable salary. If the economy or some other outside force changes the company's outlook suddenly, such a concentration of personal wealth can lead to financial disaster. Bet on your company's future, but not so much that you can't live favorably if fortunes turn. Likewise, if you're lucky enough to be invited to join another company's board of directors, take the time to understand likely strengths and weaknesses, especially those of the CEO. You don't want to take on another responsibility without realizing what baggage may come with it.

3

ADOPTING A
WORLD VIEW

IF THERE WAS A LIMIT to the number of students accepted to HBS
from foreign countries, it was not formalized. The class of 1970
had 10% of its students coming from outside North America.
These people were generally male and older, with more work experience, than the class as a whole. A dean told me that choosing them
was a challenge for the school. Should an excellent student from a
poor background who showed much promise be chosen, or should
the son of a country's ruler be selected? Which student would potentially have the larger impact on a country's economy when he
returned? HBS chose some of each type.

One sub-group that had immediate challenges upon arriving
in Boston was a small number of Japanese students, several of whom
spoke no English. They were offered a special six-week program prior
to the start of school involving an intensive introduction to English.
With the HBS curriculum built around case studies of business
situations, many which contained 30 or more pages, preparing for

three classes a day required a major effort. In the late '60s, Japan was making a global push to sell its products, and many of the students were sponsored by companies in Japan. Some had left families to attend HBS and were expected to spend the summer between the first and second years working in the United States. This meant a 21-month absence from their families. As representatives of a new wave of thinking in Japan, they were eager to achieve success.

Some of these Japanese students learned faster than others. When I joked with one of them about what I referred to as "cheap Japanese goods," he quickly corrected me: "Not cheap—inexpensive!" The nuance implied by this response predicted Japanese success worldwide. Another student sat in classes trying to follow the discussion with the help of a Japanese-English dictionary. During a heated debate someone yelled, "Bullshit!" Several in the class clapped their approval. The Japanese student dutifully paged through his dictionary to find "bullshit," but failed. When he looked at me sitting next to him, I just smiled. At lunch, I told him that whenever that person who was talking in the class spoke, it was always "bullshit." He began to understand, and "bullshit" became his favorite American expression.

Although the Japanese students studied our HBS cases primarily in their own small groups, they were not socially isolated. One Saturday night there was a dance for all first-year students and their guests. My date and I were dancing when my dormitory neighbor from Japan found inspiration in the fast music and energetically joined us. The need for developing social skills as well as business knowledge was emphasized when this same individual was given his summer job assignment: learn to be a good golfer!

Upon graduation, the Japanese students returned home to jobs waiting for them. One went back to IBM/Japan, but later made an unusual career switch and joined Millipore, which was bought by Merck in 2010. He had a successful job as an executive for about 30 years. His business future, however, was sacrificed when his wife suffered a debilitating illness and needed full-time care. Without hesitation, he quit his job, moved to their married daughter's small rural town, and shared caretaker duties for his wife with his daughter. This classmate returned to our 35th reunion in Boston at the insistence of both his wife and daughter. With a smile on his face and a cheerful demeanor, he went around the room thanking those he knew for helping him succeed in business.

This experience was deeply moving to those who knew him. We asked what happened to another Japanese student who was at HBS being groomed for a leadership post at his large Japanese corporate employer. We learned this other student made it to the executive suite as a top officer, but did not become CEO. He felt embarrassed by his supposed failure, and chose not to return for reunions. As in all cultures, each individual has to decide how to deal with success or failure on his own terms.

Surviving a Currency Freeze

South America provided about a dozen of the most colorful members of the Class of 1970. The southern countries were filled with promise and danger in equal measure, but those students coming north had confidence that the troubles could be dealt with and great success achieved.

Rampant inflation, privatizations, frozen assets, property confiscations, and major political and economic instability certainly seem like poor conditions to begin one's business career. For Chilean-born Juan Coderch, however, the challenges he faced in his adopted home of Brazil after 1970 proved highly rewarding.

Juan, at age 19, hitchhiked from Santiago, Chile, to Rio de Janeiro, Brazil, and was enchanted by Rio. After he earned a master's degree in engineering in Chile and an MBA from Harvard, he joined Citibank with the understanding he would be placed in Brazil. He spent a year training in New York, and then was sent to Brazil, which at the time generated 15% of Citibank's worldwide profits. He worked as a corporate lender to large companies from Sao Paulo, was successful, and in 1975, moved to Rio. On the same day he was named head of Citibank's investment bank, there was a major building fire that killed 185 of his expected 500 employees. Many of these deaths resulted when people threw themselves from 30 stories up to avoid the intense flames. Brazil allowed Juan one week to re-group and re-open the operation with what people and papers he could find. The tragedy prompted Citibank to redesign buildings worldwide to avoid similar fires in the future.

A Saudi investment firm operating out of London was looking to invest in Brazil. In 1976, the firm offered Juan the chance to run its investments and take a 30% ownership stake. He accepted and first started a leasing company. He grew it even as inflation roared to 20% a month, and he spent much of his time moving cash to buy assets and make quick deposits. The Brazilian economy was suffering from the aftershocks following the 1973 jump in oil prices, and its inflation for 20 years was over 100% annually. The Saudi firm became less enthusiastic about Brazil's future and Juan bought out its interest for $2.5 million.

He then moved to form a brokerage company, an investment bank, and a multibank, which was allowed to do pretty much anything. This financial empire prospered until the early '90s when the Brazilian president decided inflation needed to be tamed. He froze bank deposits for three years, effectively wiping out the wealth of many previously successful businessmen. Juan turned what might have been disaster into a great success. He owed the National Development funding agency $40 million. Because investors were fleeing Brazil, he was able to buy bonds from the same agency for 30 cents on the dollar with money kept outside the country. When eventually Brazilian bonds rallied to 100 cents on the dollar, he used this $12 million bond investment to pay back his $40 million debt. He remembered, "I was lucky to be a survivor when people were getting poorer and being wiped out. About two-thirds of the nation's top businessmen were eventually ruined." He had similar success later investing in failed Korean and Russian debt instruments.

Another great opportunity came when Brazil decided to privatize companies previously run by the government with the hopes that this might help the economy. His bank took a controlling interest in the plane manufacturer Embraer. This firm later sold over 1,000 planes, many to airlines in the United States, to handle small passenger loads (19–130 passengers). Annual sales went from $250 million to $4 billion. He also invested in the privatization deal for Brazil's largest steel mill. He bought 1% of the $1.2 billion sale offering, with the price at the time representing just 2 ½ times cash flow. The company valuation grew to $13 billion. His $12 million investment grew to more than $120 million. He sold half his shares, but those he still holds generate $3 million a year in dividends. "When a country privatizes companies previously run by the government, it represents a great opportunity," he correctly observed.

Not all business dealings were successful, and a couple times he was close to bankruptcy when over-leveraged and not properly hedged. In 1988, the Brazilian government seized 70,000 acres of Amazon timberland he controlled to establish a park. For this, he was paid 5% of the timberland's value. Other financial deals were also unsuccessful. He lost millions on an investment in Chilean vineyards. Looking back, he said, "You can make money if you have power over the market, but the wine market is too fragmented, the buyers too big and powerful, and it takes too long to establish a consumer brand."

At age 70, Juan is still actively involved with his companies, which include a railroad, a rental company for railroad equipment, a locomotive and railroad car manufacturer, and firms involved with agribusiness, real estate, and petrochemicals. His involvement is generally limited to when a problem arises. He sits on no boards. He views his primary duties as selecting who's running a company, reinvesting profits, and assuring a sound capital structure. As for

Brazil, he said the trial and error movement to democracy is pretty much over now, and it's OK to invest in the country.

Success Down Under

Another small contingent of foreigners came from Australia. Whether it was the distance they traveled or the education they received at home, the six Australians were special and made quite an impression. Four of the six became Baker Scholars by finishing in the top 5% of the class on their academic records. One introduced venture capital down under. Another became managing director of the largest luxury cruise line serving Australia and Asia. One became Premier (equivalent to a governor in the United States) of New South Wales, which includes Sydney. A section mate of mine, after a brief stint on Wall Street, went back to Sydney to establish Macquarie, a globally successful investment bank. Perhaps the brightest of the group, and maybe our entire class, joined Rio Tinto, the Australian mining giant. He worked there for 15 years and some thought he'd run the company someday. Then tragedy struck. While working around his house, he fell from a ladder and became physically and mentally impaired. Therapy and time helped him recover, but he was never the same.

Nothing Ventured, Nothing Gained

Bill Ferris was among the talented group of Australians. Unlike them and many of his classmates, Bill had six years of work experience prior to HBS since he had earned an economics degree while working during the day and attending school at night. He was fascinated by the concept of venture capital, and sought out Georges Doriot, the legendary venture capitalist who founded American Research and Development Corporation (ARDC) in 1946 to help fund business startups that would hire U.S. servicemen returning from WWII. In 1968, Doriot was 69 but still close to HBS, where he had been on the faculty since 1926 until his retirement in 1966. His ARDC firm also had just seen $70,000 invested in Digital Equipment (DEC) in 1957 turn into $355 million when DEC went public in 1968. Bill asked Doriot what was the single most important key to Ken Olsen's success as founder of DEC. Doriot's answer was, "sustained attention to detail."

Keen to learn more about venture capital and entrepreneurship, Bill signed up for the New Enterprises course introduced to HBS in 1969 by professor Pat Lyle. In the same year, Bill also met David Hawkins, HBS professor of accounting who agreed to supervise Bill's second-year thesis, written as an investment memorandum to set up Australia's first venture capital firm.

After graduating as a Baker Scholar, Bill returned to Sydney in 1970 with "more courage than capability at that point." He raised $500,000, half from the United States and the rest from Australians. With this money, at the age of 25, he opened International Venture Corporation, the first venture capital firm in Australia. It was not an instant success, but it did provide Bill with the hands-on experiences of running a manufacturing business, paying creditors, and meeting weekly payrolls. Those roles were ones he assumed in handling the work-out of a troubled portfolio company which manufactured innovative yacht fittings. Bill spent seven years as CEO for this manufacturer, expanding the company's exports, acquiring niche competitors in the United Kingdom and the United States, and eventually selling the business at a profit to a larger manufacturing group.

This experience was to prove invaluable for Bill's career in private equity, providing real-world immersion into what it's like on both sides of the desk, as investor and as an operating CEO.

On the back of this success with niche manufacturing exports, Bill was invited by the Australian government to head up its newly formed trade promotion entity, Austrade. He was the non-executive chair of this entity for almost ten years. In 1987, he and a friend formed a general partnership, Australian Mezzanine Investments, which raised the first institutionally subscribed private equity in Australia. The $30 million fund was a pioneer of small buy-outs and delivered 30% annual returns to the limited partners. This early track record led to several subsequent funds dealing with new ventures, expansion capital, and buy-outs.

The latest fund was a $1.5 billion buy-out fund focused on private equity deals in Australia and Southeast Asia. The New York-based private equity firm Castle Harlan (CHI) was a 25% affiliate partner in the general partner known as CHAMP Private Equity. The founders of CHI, John Castle and Leonard Harlan, were also HBS grads. This affiliation began in 2000 and helped the Aussies access U.S. pension funds. Thus, Bill and his team were able to lead the way in bringing offshore funds into private equity investment in Australia.

Bill sits on the HBS Asia-Pacific Advisory Board and in 2008, was made Companion in the Order of Australia (Australia's highest civilian order) for his philanthropic activities, which included support of medical research, and also for his role in establishing the private equity sector in Australia. He has written two books about investing: "Nothing Ventured Nothing Gained," and more recently, "Inside Private Equity." Each book champions the need for new venture and buy-out investments. Both books are candid about mistakes made. His current passion is for medical research to fight cancer. He is chairman of the Garvan Institute of Medical Research in Australia and recently completed a $120 million fundraising campaign to build a translational cancer research center in Sydney. This center was opened last year and is leading the push in Australia for the development of post-genomic precision medicines.

When asked what makes a successful investment, Bill said simply that "people make the difference." When he considered his major successes, he noted that those running the businesses "had a sustained attention to detail as well as a broad, forward-looking understanding of strategic positioning. They know all about their competitors and they are always inside the heads of their customers."

What would he have done differently? "I should have disciplined myself to work in an established venture capital firm in the United States after HBS and delayed my own startup by five years or so. But who knows, maybe I would have just made different mistakes!"

CRUISING AHEAD

For most of the foreigners wanting to work in the United States after graduating from HBS, their time was limited by visa restrictions. Ted Blamey graduated in 1970 and drove across the United States for three months before joining Bristol Myers as a brand manager. He did this for about a year and a half until his visa required him to leave. He stayed with Bristol Myers, first in Sydney, Australia, and then in Auckland, New Zealand. He then moved back to Sydney as head of the Clairol (hair care) division for Australia. While there, he had to fire a subordinate in sales who was older than he was and wouldn't accept direction from his younger boss.

In 1975, he joined McKinsey as a consumer marketing expert and worked on transportation, forest products, and mining studies. He finally got a consumer assignment to reposition and price products for Sitmar Cruises, which was considering shutting down. Ted offered his advice and was asked to take the managing director's job, which he turned down twice before accepting at age 32. Over seven years, he boosted Sitmar's market share from 30% to 66% and was moved to Los Angeles as CEO of the worldwide company. There, he increased the fleet and then sold the company to Princess Cruise Lines. He set up his own firm dealing with travel agents, but returned to Sydney as chairman of Sydney's Port Authority for two years. He also did some consulting work with Silversea, another luxury cruise line, and turned down an opportunity to be its president.

Ted's advice to managers: "Have a clear view as to what your business stands for and what it's good at. Be really cost conscious. Leading people is the most important thing we do as executives. You have to delegate, lead and motivate."

A FREE LUNCH

Another Australian success story was generated by Tony Berg, one of my 94 section mates sharing first-year experiences together. Tony, a Baker Scholar, went to work on Wall Street during his first summer and was quick to show initiative. He rounded up a group of ten like-minded HBS Wall Street summer employees and sent out letters to the heads of the major Wall Street firms asking them individually to lunch with the group to share their perspectives on the finance industry. When each of them agreed, Tony knew he had a problem. Paying for the lunches in a suitable setting was beyond the reach of the students. Fortunately, each leader suggested lunch at his firm's dining room or his club's restaurant or picked up the check, so the group received elegant free lunches as well as advice.

The contacts also made it easier for the participants to seek permanent employment a year later. Only one lunch caught the group off-guard. The author of a best-selling book on Wall Street accepted an invitation to speak but afterwards ran off to catch a plane, leaving the bill with the group. The students were able to collect just enough to cover the costs and leave a small tip.

After graduation, Tony joined Loeb Rhoades in New York, spending two years there before going back to Australia to join Hill Samuel, a British-owned merchant bank with a Sydney branch. He stayed at this post for 12 years as the Sydney office grew from 30 people to 200 and he became managing director in 1984. The next year, he helped found and became CEO of Macquarie Bank, an Australian merchant bank 30% owned by Hill Samuel with $50 million of newly raised capital. He ran Macquarie for nine years before deciding he shouldn't stick around too long, especially because he had an excellent successor waiting in the wings. He voluntarily stepped aside.

Tony then became CEO in 1994 of Sydney-based Boral, a $3 billion (Australian) market cap building products company with 24,000 employees worldwide. This was a turnaround situation demanding a focus on managing costs vs. managing revenues as he would in a growth situation. He did this successfully and then diversified into the energy business with an $860 million acquisition, since building products had limited pricing power. In 2000, he split apart the building materials and the energy businesses, moving himself out of a job in the process. Tony's philosophy: "I believe passionately in developing a successor. One should never fear stepping aside."

At age 55, Tony joined Gresham Partners, a boutique investment bank involving real estate, private equity, and investment banking. He spends about 50% of his time at Gresham, 20% helping nonprofit companies aid aboriginal Australians, and the remaining 30% on art, music, and corporate governance issues. His advice to business leaders is to decline doing things that don't make sense, even if others are critical of such a response. He also suggested identifying what's key to any business you're involved in and making sure it's one of your strengths before taking on an assignment.

GETTING THINGS DONE

Nick Greiner was another Australian who graduated as a Baker Scholar and left his mark on his adopted homeland. From 1988 to 1992, he was Premier (like a governor) of the Australian state of New South Wales, which includes Sydney. Both his rise and eventual fall from that position were surprising to those following Australian politics and show the degree to which luck can affect a career path.

Nick was born in Budapest, Hungary, to a Hungarian/Slovak couple working in the lumber business. The family moved to Australia, where Nick finished an economics degree before being accepted at Harvard. His father wanted him to follow into the family lumber business, so he turned down a lucrative offer from a Boston consulting firm and joined Boise Cascade. His mother-in-law was prompted to ask him, "Do you know anyone who has ever come back from Boise, Idaho?" The position did help him learn the lumber business, and over 18 months he visited 40 states trying to buy lumber yards and related businesses for Boise Cascade.

In 1972, Nick returned to Australia and helped his father's lumber business do a public offering. While in Sydney, he dabbled in politics by attending Liberal Party meetings. He had an interest in running things, and wanted to get things done. In 1980, he won an election. For the next three years, he was a junior politician while working in his father's business. In 1983, at the age of 35, he was elected leader of the Liberal Party (like the conservative Republican Party in the United States) in New South Wales. The area was a labor stronghold and there had been eight different Liberal Party leaders in eight years. He admitted he was under-prepared, but said, "It's not smart to say it's not my time."

During the 1988 election, the soon-to-be ex-premier was embroiled in an abuse of power situation, and Nick took the opportunity to run and win the premier title in New South Wales. He quickly went about privatizing things and putting the state's finances in order. In 1991, with a global recession going on, he won reelection as premier with a one-seat margin. One of the things he did was establish a Corruption Commission to assure honest government. Unfortunately for him, he had appointed an independent politician to a bureaucratic government position. His opponents challenged this move, saying it was done to allow the Liberal Party to gain that parliamentary seat. They asked the Corruption Commission to investigate Nick. While Australia's Supreme Court eventually ruled he had done nothing wrong, Nick resigned his position prior to the decision to allow the Liberal Party to retain the leadership post.

Nick left politics behind and resumed his business career. He was offered a significant number of positions as board director and accepted ten. Included in these were the board running the Australian Olympics (year 2000) and the Australian arm of British American Tobacco. For the last 20-plus years, he has enjoyed various business ventures and avoided putting all his eggs in one basket. He also mentored a lot of young people.

When asked to comment on American politics, he noted how difficult it is to take the reformist role. He had this to say about the United States presidency: "The most important position in the world (the presidency) is competed for by people who are very ordinary. American politics seem to favor the lowest common denominator. I guess that's like politics throughout the world."

STRIKING A DEAL

Dealing with political controversy is not restricted to politicians. Businesses also get involved, whether they want to or not. Such was the challenge facing Amos Schocken, an Israeli who in 1973 became general manager of the newspaper *Haaretz*. This newspaper, sometimes referred to as "The New York Times of Israel," was started in Palestine in 1919. In 1935, Amos's father bought the paper and was running it when Israel became a nation in 1948. It continued as a family operation when Amos was sent to Harvard Business School. He remained in the United States after graduation on an 18-month visa to work in finance for Fairchild Publications, which was being acquired by Capital Cities.

After this work stint, Amos's father asked him to return to Israel to replace the retiring general manager of *Haaretz*. He moved to its Tel Aviv offices and was soon tested by four labor unions that prevented the paper from being published with a series of strikes. Amos had little success in dealing with the unions, so he responded by creating new weekly newspapers in Jerusalem and Haifa and later in 12 other cities. Each of these papers had no unions. In 1984, he finally got the unions to agree to a two-tier labor contract that provided more flexibility in implementing changes.

During the '90s, the papers prospered as an influx of immigrants from Russia and a high-tech boom in Israel pushed daily subscribers to 60,000. In 2000, however, a columnist wrote about the Palestinian plight and the paper took a position in favor of the partition of Israel and Palestine. The company quickly lost 15% of its subscribers.

Amos rebuilt subscriber interest with websites offering business and technology news to complement the newspapers. A German company bought a 25% interest, with the Schocken family keeping 75%. Amos pointed out that 19% of Israel's inhabitants are Arabs, with 90% of these Muslims, so religions need to work together. "*Haaretz* is a newspaper with a mission," he said. "We have a vision of what the country should be." He takes a controversial stance with the paper's policy because he feels he must. The paper supports: (1) a Zionist position endorsing the existence of Israel as a Jewish and democratic state; (2) a high level of civil and human rights with freedom from coercion; (3) improvements in education, science, and culture; (4) individual expression; (5) a market economy; and (6) peace between Israel and Arab nations.

As for the future, Amos believes *Haaretz* will prosper by providing news both over the internet and in print. He said he feels a heavy responsibility to help Israel in his role as a key formulator of public opinion. With a pragmatic and well-reasoned approach to the challenges both the paper and the country face, he is likely to succeed.

HARD CHOICES

Everyone pursuing a business career faces difficult choices somewhere along the way. Do I want to accept a job in a geographic area I'm not familiar with or not enthusiastic about? Am I willing to move to a different location if asked as my career progresses? What about uprooting the family, or asking a spouse to leave his/her job to follow? What do I do if I've chosen the wrong company, or find it moving in the wrong direction? How do I get myself out of a situation where I have a bad boss or am asked to violate my personal principles or ethics? Do I have to sacrifice my family life or personal interests to achieve career success? Graduating from HBS doesn't exempt you from the hard choices.

Christian Lesur joined a major European chemical company in a key treasury position and returned to his native France. He reported to the CFO and played a role in establishing a centralized treasury function and revamping the group's finances. Four years later, he was promoted to manager of strategy for the newly formed agricultural division of this chemical company, and helped the unit become a world class player in agrochemicals and a leading profit contributor.

In 1977, facing conflict with top management over a product strategy and financial trouble at the parent company, Christian left to join Nestle. He rapidly became deputy treasurer and head of corporate finance, moving from Paris to Switzerland even though his new wife had a Paris-based career. This move worked well for a while as the couple had two children and Christian was assigned to headquarters in Vevey, just outside of Geneva. In 1983, his success prompted a promotion and a request to move to the United States for Nestle. His wife refused to move, and he faced difficult choices: move to the United States and face family disruption; stay at headquarters and face lesser career prospects; or move back to Paris and look for a job. He chose the family, left Nestle, and returned to Paris.

In Paris, he made the somewhat hasty decision to join a large and well-known chemical/pharmaceutical company. He was soon confronted by arguing shareholders as well as the firm's inbred culture and inability to accept outsiders. Over the next two years, he nevertheless did substantial business development work and was promoted to deputy CFO overseeing several merger and acquisition projects. This led him in 1987 to join Bank BNP in the mergers and acquisitions area, where for the next 13 years he advised on many European cross-border transactions. He left following BNP's acquisition of Bank Paribas when the latter provided the management leadership in his business area.

In 2001, he joined a diversified industrial and mining firm, heading strategy and development as one of three key executives. Five years later, he retired to do strategic and financial consulting on his own. Christian now sits on two family-owned company corporate boards and advises family-owned businesses and entrepreneurial ventures.

Reflecting on his long career, he offered several thoughts for those starting out in business:

(1) *Marriage may be the most important decision you have to make. Compatibility and willingness to compromise can make the difference between success and an average business performance.* Christian's marriage and joining Nestle were intrinsically incompatible and resulted in a dreadful choice: divorce with two small children or leaving Nestle at a critical time in his career development.

(2) *Network fully but carefully.* Christian praised HBS's worldwide reach and high quality, but warned that an HBS degree is no guarantee of either professionalism or honesty.

(3) *In the end, basic business economics apply: bubbles burst, and radically new ideas dissipate.* Christian remembered the HBS year 2000 reunion dinner where he was told that "our kids have created a new economy, and we have become old."

(4) *Democracy is essentially unstable and at times unpredictable, requiring care and high ethics from its elites, including its business elites, if acceptance of wealth is to remain.*

(5) *The challenge ahead is greater than it has ever been. The world is a fast-changing and fragile place. This is not a time for shortsightedness.* As Albert Einstein put it: "We shall require a substantially new manner of thinking if mankind is to survive."

COMMUNISM TO CAPITALISM

Sometimes working in a foreign culture requires you to forget the laws of society and adapt to the laws of the jungle. It can be an unfair and harsh world out there, far away from the comforts of Harvard. You need to adapt in order to survive.

Not all the international business lessons were learned by foreigners. Some of the most interesting challenges overseas confronted home-grown Americans who ventured outside their comfort zones. One who took a chance was Jack Stack, long-time New York City banker who suddenly found himself working in the communism-to-capitalism cauldron that was the new Czech Republic.

Most of Jack Stack's professional career was pretty normal. He worked as an aid to NYC Mayor John Lindsay after he graduated from HBS. He then joined the city's court system in a financial capacity to help the courts reorganize. Employment as a retail banker for 22 years followed, first at Chemical Bank and then at Chase, which acquired Chemical. After 30 years in New York City, Jack was feeling comfortable. Then the phone rang.

In February, 2000, Jack was recruited by the Austrian Erste Bank to become CEO of the largest bank in the Czech Republic. Erste Bank had agreed to acquire the Czech bank (Ceska Sporiteina) from the government, which had decided to privatize it while moving from communism towards capitalism. The Austrians weren't sure that one of their own employees would be accepted, and existing Czech employees made loans with an unusual approach that was not conducive to good banking. Jack had some small business lending experience to go with his retail background, and his American training made him a neutral choice.

Jack flew to Prague to begin work. He quickly learned that the bank's purchase allowed Erste Bank to return loans to the government not deemed acceptable, and 45% of the loans fell in the non-performing or delinquent category. He discovered the customary practice was for the borrower to kickback 6% of a loan to the lending officer. A $100,000 loan would allow the individual lender to put $6,000 into his personal pocket. Jack's first task was to stop that practice and return most of the bad loans to the government.

For a bank its size, 10,000 employees were a more suitable number than the 15,000 Jack inherited. Equally important, people who grew up under communism had trouble adjusting to capitalistic business practices. He reduced head-count and had remaining employees sign a simple, two-page code of conduct to make sure everyone knew there would be no tolerance for any sign of corruption. Because everyone knew the failed bank needed a transformation, he was helped in making changes. He recruited locally for new employees, but looked for people under 40 who had worked outside Austria and the Czech Republic. The average age of the bank's managing board was only 34.

Jack viewed the transformation as a political process. He campaigned for targets that were understandable and acceptable to both employees and customers. For example, the ATMs were repeatedly failing, so he announced publicly that all would be fixed over the next four quarters. He also had to adjust to certain cultural differences. A politician wanted him to make a certain loan, which he rejected. When warned that might not be a good idea, he joked, "I'm petrified," and his staff thought he was serious.

In three years, the bank went from four to five million customers and loans grew from 30% of the deposit base to 70%, yielding an 18% ROE (return on equity). Jack had planned to stay on the job for three years, but he remained for seven before returning to

New York. He's glad he grabbed the opportunity for a new experience, and remains on the Austrian bank's board of directors, flying to Vienna five to six times a year for meetings. He's also on the boards of Allied Financial (the old GMAC) and Mutual of America (with $17 billion under management). He encouraged people to welcome challenges in their careers, and not to fear changes. "It's important to broaden your experiences, even if this means moving laterally to do so," he said.

POWER TO THE PEOPLE

Another American classmate dragged into a socialist system and making his work a success, at least initially, was Dennis Bakke. In the process, his business path moved from bureaucrat to consultant to billionaire and then to scapegoat, finally switching to a new career running charter schools in the United States.

Taking what you're given and making a success of it is the goal of every entrepreneur, but the path is generally not smooth. Such was the case for Dennis, who grew up financially poor and went to college courtesy of a football scholarship. After HBS, he spent six years working for the federal government in Washington, D.C., the final two years in the Federal Energy Administration. At the time, the FEA was run by John Sawhill, a strong advocate of energy conservation after the Arab oil embargo of 1974. Dennis was his assistant, working on ideas to improve and conserve energy. When the FEA began aggressively pushing a gasoline tax on American consumers, Sawhill was fired and Dennis left to start an energy think tank at Carnegie Mellon University in Pittsburgh.

Dennis enjoyed his consulting, but after a few years he wanted something more. He and Roger Saut joined together in 1981 to launch Applied Energy Sources (AES). This independent utility built small and efficient electric plants, using coal to make steam and generate electricity, then selling the steam to industrial firms and the electricity to the "grid" for other utilities to use. The favorable economics of the process led to rapid growth, and seven plants were built in five years. Not content with this progress, the company began buying inefficient utilities outside the U.S. These purchases included, in 1989, one of the biggest energy plants in the world—a 4,000-megawatt giant in Kazakhstan that was then operating at only 10% efficiency.

Corruption and employees who worked little and were paid poorly offered a challenge to the new owners. Dennis implemented his own philosophy: empower people by trusting them. "It's all about the people," he thought, and pushed down decision-making to the lowest possible level. Improvement was rapid, and the same approach was used to buy on the cheap and turn around some 15 other international power facilities. Purchases included facilities in India, China, Brazil, Argentina, Venezuela, parts of Africa, and various Third World countries.

AES, which had gone public in 1991, was wonderfully successful by following four major principles: act with integrity, be fair, have fun, and be socially responsible. By 2002, the company had 40,000 employees and $8.6 billion in annual revenue. Dennis's paper net worth was then over $2 billion. Unfortunately, cracks in the system were beginning to show.

As production of electricity became more efficient and less costly, governments in the United States and especially in less developed parts of the world began demanding lower consumer prices. The successes that had been achieved were now being used to penalize AES. The stock price dropped, the company went through a major restructuring, and Dennis retired after pressure from his board of directors.

The story has a happy ending because with time again available to him, he and his wife started a private Christian school. They named the new venture Imagine Schools, and in its first seven years, it developed into the largest charter school organization in the United

States with 76 public schools and 45,000 students. The system was privately run in friendly competition with public schools. Dennis is adamant that parents (his customers) be treated with respect and that they should decide what schools their children attend.

When asked to comment on his business career, Dennis said: "Our people were fantastic. The boards were the problem. You have to be prepared to lose your job if you're the CEO. Every board vote is unanimous, but if things go bad, the CEO is blamed." He also observed, "The corporation is there to serve others, and shareholders aren't necessarily served first. You have to balance employees, governments, customers, etc. All should be treated with equal respect."

Cash Flow Is King

James Lees came to HBS almost by accident. He attended Great Britain's Cranfield School of Management and while there, applied for and won an Eisenhower Fellowship to tour the United States for six months and explore a topic of his choosing. He picked venture capital and private equity investing. While touring, he came to HBS to speak with a professor who talked him into coming to HBS in the fall of 1969 for a second year of business school. That fall, Harvard took six people from Cranfield, each entering the second year of the MBA program with enough credits from Cranfield to bypass the first year.

James was 31 years old at the time and not sure he wanted to enter another academic program rather than get a job. He also wasn't sure that bypassing HBS's first year, when all classes were held with the same people and friendships were formed, was a good idea. In the second year, each class had different people, so it was harder to connect with others. He came anyway and when finished, found that visa restrictions made it necessary for him to return to Great Britain. He took a job in London at the financial conglomerate Slater Walker Securities. When it went bust in the economic turmoil of 1973, he turned to property development. His real interest was doing leveraged capital buyouts, on which he had written a paper, but at that time it wasn't being done in Britain. He was too early.

Since as a youth he had spent time living in the Middle East and could speak Arabic, he decided to move to Dubai and with some other Brits, began building residential homes for senior executives of foreign firms. They were not allowed to buy land, but could own 12 to 15-year leaseholds. Once a home was built, it could be rented out. A French-Arab bank provided 100% of the funds needed, and the company built 150 estates in Dubai and 250 elsewhere in the Middle East. Returns were a hefty 30% per year, and James was doing well but not getting rich enough to retire. When in 1980 locals who could own land started doing the same building/renting of homes that he had pioneered, he knew it was time to move on.

Back in London, he worked as a consultant in resort development, helping a British company reorganize a 1,000-acre Spanish resort. He also worked on a golf development in southern France and another in southern Spain. "Resorts are very cyclical," he said, "and you have to have deep pockets." He structured partnerships with a separate company to do each development. Cash flow was king, so when the market weakened in 1994, he sat out the next five years. He went to Hong Kong to try to form a timeshare program, but another downturn made him decide to return to the United Kingdom. The Lehman investment firm collapse in 2008 stopped an idea for promoting shared exclusive properties and destination resorts, so in 2009, he returned funds already raised and retired.

Looking back at his career, he was happy he chose the entrepreneurial route. "It was riskier but more satisfying," he said. "A lot of success is just timing—this is of the essence. Timing and luck are the keys. You have to be willing to sit it out for a while if markets are unfavorable. I could have made more money working in finance, but I had fun doing what I did. I stayed light, and with no overhead, I could do things on my own."

Logical Logistics

In the late '60s, a popular film (The Graduate) advised the main character to key in on "plastics." For Sam Schotsky, his career anticipated the future with a more modern focus on "logistics." His interest began after college when his ROTC training took him to France in 1965 to work in the Army's Transportation Corps. He became a valued assistant to a full colonel who ultimately went to Vietnam. Sam continued in Europe while most of his group's senior officers went to Vietnam.

Sam left the Army in early 1967 and worked in freight forwarding for a small company before applying to HBS. Despite what he called "a miserable academic record" while at Boston University, "two glowing personal recommendations" got him into the Class of 1970. There is no doubt in Sam's view that his education at HBS gave him a set of tools he has used ever since. Especially valuable was the ability to analyze and evaluate business opportunities, and to be able to see and understand the many sides of complex issues.

After graduation, he got a job in the brand-new planning department at the airline Pan Am. He quickly learned that he didn't want to work for a large company burdened by politics and bureaucracy. He went back into freight forwarding for 35 years, moving from New York City to Los Angeles to Miami, back to LA, and finally to Atlanta. An early focus was transporting pharmaceutical products between Puerto Rico and the United States mainland. From the early '90s until 2008, Sam was heavily involved with China and later in his career, he and his Chinese partners created a logistics company involving China, the United States, and the rest of the world.

Sam believes management often doesn't appreciate how logistics can make an operation succeed or fail. He remembers when a Fortune 500 firm sent electronics by air to the Middle East, thus paying ten times the cost of moving the same goods by ship. They sat at the destination and deteriorated. Why? Management couldn't book the merchandise as sold until it landed at its destination, so it was sent by air to meet sales targets.

Another time, circuit boards were sent to Egypt where officials not only opened the containers but also opened the sealed circuit boards themselves, ruining the shipment. The officials were expecting "facilitation fees" for not interfering, but paying such fees would be viewed in the United States as illegal bribery. "Sometimes a United States business is severely handicapped in dealing with certain countries when trying to get a job done," Sam observed. Some firms get a local business partner to deal with the local practices and customs and stay out of the way.

His advice for handling international trade was not to "define a problem too tightly and keep a bigger perspective on what's going on." He advised people to get heavily involved in the foreign countries where they work, and learn at least 10–20 words prior to going there for the first time to show respect for the culture. "This familiarization can be the best investment you can make."

A PURE THINKER

The admissions department at HBS tends to favor people who are doers rather than true intellectuals when building a class, and the Class of 1970 was no exception. A rugby captain, football and basketball All-Americans, war heroes, and IBM's leading salesman (a non-college grad) were all admitted. H. Woody Brock, however, came to HBS as a pure thinker with a sense of adventure.

Woody earned an undergraduate degree from Harvard as well as a master's degree in political theory and math with an emphasis on decision theory. He went to speak to faculty member Tony Athos, instrumental at HBS in choosing potential students, and said he wanted to work on his MBA but first wanted to get away from everything. This he did by spending four months in Papua, New Guinea, where Nelson Rockefeller's son Michael had disappeared just five years earlier. At the time, there was speculation that Michael might have been eaten. Woody arrived at HBS in the fall of 1968 ready for anything.

Upon graduating from HBS, he continued studying at Princeton and earned an M.A. and Ph.D. in mathematical economics and political philosophy. With five degrees from two prestigious educational institutions and teachers who included two Nobel prize-winners in economics, Woody used decision theory to help predict how economics might be applied in times of uncertainty. He became a consultant and internationally noted speaker on various economic topics. He was especially welcomed at global corporations, political gatherings, hedge funds, banks, and world economic forums. He was noted for spotting structural changes in international economies and doing risk assessment for various global asset classes.

He published many articles in professional journals and has written several *New York Times* Op-Ed pieces. In 2012, his newest book was published: "American Gridlock—Why the Right and Left Are Both Wrong, Commonsense 101 Solutions to the Economic Crisis." The book identified five issues challenging the United States and offered possible solutions. The issues discussed included: the current slow growth and high unemployment of this decade (2011–2020); the entitlement crisis; the possibility of future financial market meltdowns; the need to bargain effectively with China and what he called "thugocracies;" and the need to salvage capitalism by deciding who gets how much and why.

Woody spends about four months a year traveling to consult and give speeches. His personal passion is collecting "Golden Age" (1670–1800) objects from England and France. He recently donated a collection containing his European works of art to the Museum of Fine Arts in Boston.

WIPE OUT

John Bradlow's parents had thrived in the British colony of Rhodesia in southern Africa, amassing buildings and other real estate, which gave them a comfortable living. In 1965, the conservative white minority government declared Rhodesia independent of Britain, prompting a 15-year guerilla war with the black majority. The family moved to South Africa and was there when, after a 1980 peace agreement, Robert Mugabe became president of Rhodesia, renamed Zimbabwe. President Mugabe quickly moved against non-native Africans, confiscating property and heavily taxing what remained. Currency controls prevented removing funds from the country, and the rents the Bradlow family had been collecting had to remain in bank accounts as massive inflation destroyed the economic value of the currency. "Civilization has a thin veneer," John observed.

John realized his family fortunes were being wiped out, and applied in 1968 to Harvard Business School. He was accepted, and remembers how different things were in the United States. An early HBS case study discussed the benefits of 30-second vs. 60-second spot commercials for TV advertising. Since there was no television in South Africa in 1968, he didn't know what his classmates were talking about. After graduation, he returned to South Africa. Although it was a democracy, the country had high levels of crime and an uncertain future for English-speaking white citizens. John decided to immigrate to Canada in 1976. Because people like him were discouraged from leaving South Africa, he had to leave his money behind.

He arrived in Montreal in 1977, broke at age 32 and with a wife and two children. Fortunately, his MBA degree from Harvard helped him get a job at the Bank of Montreal, where he spent a dozen years helping companies get financing. At age 45, he was offered a promotion that would have put him among the top five officers of the bank. He would, however, have to sign a five-year employment contract. "I knew I wasn't the type of person who thrived in a bureaucratic system," John said. He turned down the promotion and joined what he described as a financial "wheeling and dealing firm" that went bust two years later.

He next joined a private equity fund as its sole owner. Six years later, he sold it and two years after that, he bought it back again and grew it from $50 million to $350 million in assets. The firm, named Pen Fund, did half its business in the United States and half in Canada, targeting up to $50 million per deal.

John reflected on corporate life and was glad he went his own way, despite the handicap of not having a paycheck. "To get to the top of the apex in a corporate setting, political adroitness is the required thing," he said. "But the emotional hardening you need is far more difficult than most think. You see friends embittered or pushed into retirement. You don't feel fulfilled. With the entrepreneurial choice you have more control over your own life, and the road is a happier one."

CONSULTING FOR BIG OIL

Over 30 years as an international consultant has provided David Brown with some unique perspectives on how the world works, in his specialty of oil and gas drilling and oil field services. For example, the government of Brazil mandated that 16 new drilling rigs to explore off-shore waters were to be built by 2016 in the country, even though nobody had ever built a drilling rig in Brazil before. The international companies that were best equipped to help all refused to participate, so the government told the state-controlled oil firm Petrobras to make it happen.

Another time, in Mexico, a drilling rig went idle because a part broke. The part could be air-freighted in, but it would arrive after the airport nearby closed at 6:00 p.m. The airport manager said, "just pay the overtime" to keep the airport open. This was done and the United States Justice Department investigated David under the Foreign Corrupt Practices Act to determine whether this constituted bribery and was thus illegal. David said the biggest problem was immigration related. The United States and Canada were very strict in not accepting payment for work permits for foreign workers. Other countries accepted such payments, and companies could more easily schedule their foreign workers.

David began his consulting career in 1970 with the Boston Consulting Group. One of his early assignments was working for Shell in Brazil. He was then moved to London to help Shell launch development of the North Sea for drilling. He returned to the United States in 1977 and spent a brief stint as director of strategic planning for Teradyne before going back to consulting with Braxton, which was sold in 1984 to what is now Deloitte-Touche. He left soon after to start his own consulting firm in Boston, the Windsor Group, specializing in strategy for oil field service companies.

As president for over 20 years at the Windsor Group, he was asked to join the boards of Layne Christensen (a billion-dollar mineral company), and Pride International (the second largest deepwater drilling company). In 2011, Pride was acquired by Ensco (an oil and gas drilling and exploration company on the New York Stock Exchange). He served as audit chairman of Ensco and chairman of the Layne board. He now advocates strongly the separation of chairman and CEO roles. He also said the Sarbanes Oxley legislation has "absolutely killed the CPAs," who are now "afraid of their shadows." He added, "You can't consult with them. They always have to check with their bosses."

GLOBAL LEGAL ISSUES

The Vietnam War influenced the planning of many classmates. For Clark McFadden, his ROTC service in college allowed him only a two-year deferment for further study, so he enrolled at HBS to get an MBA. While completing his first year, he learned about a joint business/law degree that Harvard offered on a total four-year program. When he got the Navy's approval, he continued on for three more years and got both business and law school degrees.

Luckily for Clark, HBS Professor Robert Anthony had been a roommate of Robert McNamara, U.S. Secretary of Defense under Presidents Kennedy and Johnson. With Prof. Anthony's endorsement, Clark was sent to a special analysis group at the Pentagon, followed by a stint on the National Security Council staff at the White House, and then moved to a job as a general counsel to the Senate Armed Services Committee. When he finished his service in 1976, he easily transitioned into legal practice on international trade issues.

"The legal profession has become quite global," according to Clark. "The American legal system dominates international law, but it's not the only country to have an impact. There are a lot of different legal traditions, conventions, and codes. A lot of negotiation is used in reaching a decision." Frequent issues of law involve regulations, international transactions, investigations (such as bribery, money laundering, etc.), and unfair trade practices.

Clark personally won a steel dumping case against Japan by proving that government financing for a company gave it an unfair advantage. "But it's hard to stop such cases since in many countries the steel industry is a symbol of strength," he explained, and special favors are expected. He also helped the U.S. semi-conductor industry prosper by forcing other countries to allow U.S. companies to compete. "Japan used to be the main challenge, but now China is. There's still theft of intellectual property. The Chinese have laws that are OK, but the implementation of these laws is lacking." Even Canada, by subsidizing its timber exports, is making it difficult to keep U.S. lumber competitive. "Worldwide, however, there is less formal protectionism than there was 25 years ago."

For those seeking a career in international regulation and trade, there's no well-defined path. "A broad-based educational background is worthwhile," Clark said. "You also need to be innovative, resourceful, and entrepreneurial to be successful. At the same time, you must understand the mechanics of the bureaucracy and be able to respond appropriately."

4

Doing Business
Worldwide

THERE ISN'T ENOUGH TIME FOR HBS to prepare students for all
the surprises that may come with an international business
career. Currency controls, differing customs and ethics, work
visa restrictions, language barriers, uncertain legal frameworks, corruption, expropriation, etc.—all might be factors that affect business
decisions. The best Harvard can do is to emphasize preparing well
and remaining flexible to deal with problems as they occur.

One of the most challenging events mentioned in the previous section is the example of Brazil and Zimbabwe (formerly
Rhodesia), where bank accounts were frozen and inflation ruined
the value of assets held. Unusual to be sure, but poor economies
can prompt political leaders to take extreme steps to confiscate
wealth. Could it happen in the United States? Such steps are hard
to imagine here, but the United States has financial obligations
(Social Security and Medicare/Medicaid, for example) that have
been promised but are unlikely to be delivered as costs escalate.

Might the dollar eventually become a political target and devalued to allow payment of all our promised commitments? It could happen here, as it might happen in a variety of other countries. The best strategy is to diversify investments and business assets on an international basis to provide some protection.

The rule of law is an important consideration in where a business should be located. Expropriation of private property has occurred in the past and might again. Is adequate and fair compensation paid? What about situations such as buying major power plants in Third World countries, making them efficient, and having the value diminished by governments demanding lower electric rates for local customers? What should be done when China has laws protecting intellectual property rights but does not enforce these laws if secrets can be gained from foreign companies? How do you compete as a landlord when a foreigner cannot own land on which to build houses but a local resident can? Such issues should be considered before making business and investment decisions.

Another international question is how to handle bribery issues in places where such payments are commonly used to get things done. If you own circuit boards that are not only stopped upon arrival but actually taken apart because "facilitation fees" aren't paid to customs agents, how should you respond? Paying such fees might be violating the foreign corrupt practices act that the United States enforces. What about paying overtime to Mexican airport workers to keep an airport open until a critical part can be flown in? The United States views this action as a bribery issue. One possible approach is to have a local partner responsible for getting things done as necessary without your support, knowledge, or involvement. Sometimes skirting the edge of legality is the only option open to a businessman working internationally.

There are also many social issues to be considered in an international career. Will older workers accept younger bosses? What about workers with new female bosses? Is the workforce so familiar with a different economic system (such as socialism) that it can't adapt to capitalism? If you have a family, can you accept a foreign assignment and will your family be willing to go with you? Are there private, English-speaking schools, or are local schools feasible for your children? What about visits to relatives in the United States or some other country if you're stationed far away? How about personal taxes and cost-of-living adjustments? Is there a specific time when you will be brought back to headquarters after a foreign assignment? It's much more challenging to deal with foreign assignments than those in domestic locations. Then again, understanding how differently situations are viewed by other cultures might better prepare a person for international customers and future competition.

5

Entrepreneurship

W HEN THE CLASS OF 1970 attended Harvard Business School, the school's favorable reputation was based on its history of training future top managers for large companies. Most of us thought we were destined for bigness, if not greatness. While a few grads did follow the large company career path, most of us found, to our surprise, that the corporate upheavals and reorganizations of the '70s made the single employer a thing of the past. Opportunism was what moved you ahead, not loyalty. We quickly learned to take advantage of change, not fear it.

Ironically, around 1968–69 there were few opportunities to learn such individualistic approaches in the classroom. There were only two HBS teachers devoted to entrepreneurship. Today, there are 45, or 15% of the faculty. There is now a required first-year course called "The Entrepreneurial Manager." Second-year students devote 40% of their classroom hours studying entrepreneurship and related subjects.

Graduates in 1970 who followed their own paths, even without formal training, usually had enough smarts and flexibility to make a success of most business ventures they took on. Entrepreneurship became a badge of honor, and a new path to personal wealth.

A VENTURE PHILANTHROPIST

Proving what could be accomplished with a can-do startup approach was Bob Higgins, a 1970 grad who early on became a venture capitalist and is now also a senior lecturer at Harvard. Bob was in the Army ROTC program, and was expecting military service upon graduation in 1970. The Vietnam War, however, was requiring fewer officers at that time, so instead Bob went to West Point as assistant director of admissions. He soon was moved to Washington in a post with the U.S. Treasury, and was later made an assistant to Commerce Secretary Peter Peterson.

After fulfilling his ROTC obligations for government service, at age 26 he became CEO of a new foundation dedicated to improving healthcare. From 1973 to 1982, he ran this and two similar foundations and discovered entrepreneurship. He described it as "venture philanthropy," looking to solve social problems with unique approaches. He helped start HBOs (health benefit organizations) that shared medical costs among many members. These included one for the Mormon Church in Utah and another that led to the founding of United Health Care. He set up hospices for the dying, and looked for better ways to manage illness. Many of these ventures began as nonprofit but became for-profit organizations.

His early successes prompted a move in 1983 to Charles River Ventures, a venture capital firm specializing in healthcare services. The firm developed new models of care such as home infusion companies. One of these, New England Critical Care, was perfected in the academic world as a nonprofit before switching to a for-profit, in the process generating more than a 30 times return for investors.

In 1988, he left to start Highland Capital Partners, which also focused on healthcare. An early success was Odyssey Health Care, a

84

hospice care firm that in five years generated a 25 times return for investors. Most of these health-related firms had the common theme of IT-enabled services, using software to improve management.

Bob bemoans the lack of cross-training for business graduates. "Society desperately needs people with government, nonprofit and business experience. You need the versatility to have a larger view. Until Watergate, great leaders had experience in government and business. But in the last 25 years, rules in Washington have become so difficult that good people don't go there—it's too unattractive for a senior person. What Washington does attract is lawyers, academics, and poor politicians."

Bob is now teaching on the faculty of Harvard's Kennedy School, trying to help philanthropy groups understand and adopt strategic purposes. His course, "Entrepreneurship in the Private, Public and Social Sectors," has 80 students, 20 of whom are MDs. Also keeping him busy is monitoring two young twins that he had soon after being married in his late 50s. "That's my number one job now," he said.

KEEPING FIT

Spotting a trend earlier than others is often the way to wealth. This was true for Jerry Dauderman, a Baker Scholar in 1970 who bounced around a bit before finding his niche in fitness gyms in southern California in 1976. Jerry had done missionary work in the Dominican Republic for two years after college before going to HBS. Upon graduation, he wasn't sure what he wanted to do, so he joined Harvard's School of Design as director of development (fundraising). This lasted just a year before he went to South America to run a company in Colombia. After two years doing that, he joined a classmate in Dallas as VP at a life insurance company that was sold two years later to a German company.

Jerry was in Dallas when he had lunch with a Nautilus fitness equipment salesman. He decided he needed to do something to cure his own overweight condition, so he bought some equipment. He liked it enough to move to California and open fitness centers. His wife Bobbi joined him in this effort and they built a large, high-end coed center to compete with the then-common sweaty gyms for men. The decision was a winner, and both sexes began regular training. From 1976 to 1992, the Daudermans opened 24 fitness centers. They then sold them to Bally's for stock, and watched with glee as Bally's stock went up three-fold before Hilton bought that company. Five physical therapy centers they had developed were also sold, to Health South.

After the fitness center sale, Jerry accepted the task of trying to resurrect a bankrupt casino operation. This job ended with the casino sold out of bankruptcy although "the lawyers milked it until all the cash was gone," he remembered. Since then, he has developed some real estate, done angel investing in small companies, and enjoyed frequent travels, often overseas. He currently is a member of the Pacific Council on International Policy (a think tank). One of his more unusual activities is working with Muslims in southern California. He is active in a Presbyterian church, and he mixes Muslims and Presbyterians by holding small dinners where they develop friendships that allow for understanding of their respective faiths and cultures.

FAILING YOUR WAY TO SUCCESS

Graduating from HBS presents something of a challenge to a would-be entrepreneur. There is almost always a lucrative job opportunity awaiting the graduate, if one wants to take it. Back in 1970, the average HBS grad had an annual salary of $15,000. Adjusted for inflation, that same salary would be the equivalent of about $100,000. Now, however, all students who enter HBS are required to have work experience prior to coming to the school. The average salary upon leaving is over $150,000 annually, but this may be misleading since many students start a company or join a startup. For those taking a high-paying job, a comfortable lifestyle is assured, at least in the immediate future. Now, as in 1970, saying no to a lucrative opportunity is not easy and requires quite a bit of self-confidence and a willingness to accept the financial risks involved. In the case of Dal LaMagna, living with a dozen years of failure made eventual success all the sweeter. After leading 15 startups and failing 15 times, he finally found a surprising niche in a surprising way.

Dal's business inspiration was as simple as a pain in the ass — literally, in the case of this founder of Tweezerman. In the late '70s, having failed as an entrepreneur in everything he tried, he was sunbathing with his girlfriend on a redwood deck in Venice Beach, California. Sunbathing led to other antics and he wound up with his backside covered with splinters. Stooping over and looking through his legs into a mirror with tweezers in one hand and a needle in the other, he was incapable of grabbing even one of the splinters. He wished he had needle-pointed tweezers for the job. His girlfriend helped out by removing 32 splinters.

A year later, Dal was working at minimum wage for an electronics firm where the workers on the assembly line were picking up capacitors and diodes with needle-pointed tweezers made in Italy. He bought some, packaged them as splinter tweezers, and sold them to hardware and lumber stores on Long Island.

A friend of Dal's, who worked in a beauty salon, asked if he could supply her with precision-pointed tweezers she could use and sell as eyebrow tweezers. Dal sourced tweezers used by jewelers for handling diamonds and thought they could also be used to pluck eyebrows. His friend started selling them like hotcakes.

Dal put the eyebrow tweezers into clear tubes and called on beauty salons on Saturdays in Manhattan. He convinced the salons to pay $10 for tweezers that cost him $4. He started making more money in one day selling Dal LaMagna Grooming Tweezers than he earned all week at his day job, so he quit the day job. When one of the salon receptionists yelled to everyone that "Tweezerman is here," Dal changed the name of his company on the spot.

The company grew with Dal delegating aggressively and focusing on beauty care implements. He had learned at HBS the importance of balancing production, sales, and control, and grew the company slowly. He made a living and after he reached $10 million in annual sales, he started making serious money. He started Tweezerman with $500, and 25 years later, with a major assist from a giant billboard seen when exiting New York City, revenues were over $25 million. He then sold the company for over $50 million to a German company looking for a specialized consumer product that could be marketed worldwide.

Dal narrates his adventures in detail in his book, "Raising Eyebrows: A Failed Entrepreneur Finally Gets It Right," where he confesses that chasing success caused him to drop out of Harvard Business School for a year and return to graduate in 1971. He always was willing to push the envelope in taking risks. When he was initially accepted to attend HBS, he received a loan to pay his tuition. Arriving a week early before the first class, he overheard a hot tip conversation and placed a bet with his tuition money on call options on Global Marine's stock. A couple weeks later, the coming good news turned out to be bad news and the stock cratered. Dal lost everything. He went to the financial aid office, told them what had happened, and pointed out (correctly) that they should have deducted the tuition immediately rather than give him the cash up front. What was said Dal wouldn't say, but he did receive another loan and was able to attend classes.

Not so successful were a couple of brief attempts Dal made at getting into politics. In 1996, he ran for Congress in the 3rd district in Nassau County (New York). He spent $1 million of his own money running against incumbent Peter King but fell short with 42% of the vote. He ran again in 2000 and lost again. In 2008, he was one of at least 30 Democratic candidates running in the New Hampshire primary for President of the United States, mainly on the strength of his opposition to the war in Iraq. He received just eight votes, most of which he attributes to personally fixing a neighborhood street pothole. "Don't go into politics," Dal advised.

Now living in New York, Dal is working to turn around IceStone, a company that makes countertops in Brooklyn out of recycled glass and cement. His strategy, to empower workers, is doing well. The company was losing $3 million annually before Dal took over, but within a year it reached break-even. When Hurricane Sandy blew away his factory, IceStone's employees rebuilt the factory with the help of a $1 million SBA disaster loan. IceStone soon reached profitability.

When asked how he empowers employees, Dal said: "Make all employees partners in the company (at IceStone they own 10%), involve them in all levels of decision making, pay them a living wage, distribute 5% of the annual profits to them, provide health and job security, teach them how the company functions, and lead them more as a professor than a dictator."

Classmate Frank Suttell shared in Dal's success by joining the Tweezerman company in 1994 as its chief financial officer. This plunge into small business followed 22 years as a consultant and a commercial banker, but also immediately followed two years working for the Peace Corps in Bulgaria. While there, he helped convert the socialist Bulgarian National Bank into six independent and private banks, moving capitalism forward and, he said, "making people much happier." While at Tweezerman, he helped introduce 12 different types of tweezers with 100 different variations into several foreign countries. He described all the tweezers as of the highest quality. He also helped establish manufacturing facilities in India. The school tie link was further used in completing the company's sale when New York attorney and HBS classmate Clark McFaddan, who held both law and MBA degrees from Harvard, was hired to do the legal work.

TONS OF FUN

While financial gain is what most people think of when they start a successful company, most entrepreneurs are more pleased with the personal freedom success allows and the chance to be creative in a helpful way. Taking full advantage of all opportunities was Lance Funston, who almost didn't make it to his second year at HBS because of his entrepreneurial pursuits.

If you rearrange Lance Funston's last name and add a couple letters, you wind up with "tons of fun." That is a pretty good description of Lance's life after graduation, and as a serial entrepreneur, he worked hard to keep it that way. He's the one who introduced you to "8-minute abs," "instant flower garden," and "the super-soaker" via cable TV's infomercials, making himself rich in the process. He also threatened the pros at the 2005 U.S. Poker Championship by being the first day's chip leader even though it was only his second tournament ever. He finished 22nd out of 420 competitors. He played his way to a top-20 ranking as a croquet player, and at age 50, took up bobsledding and participated as an alternate in the 1994 Olympics in Norway.

Lance was surprised by his acceptance to HBS even though he had won four national debating titles before graduating in 1967 from the University of Houston. He had worked briefly as an assistant to the director of the FDIC (Federal Deposit Insurance Corporation) and as an assistant to a governor of the Federal Reserve Board. During the summer before entering Harvard, he worked with John Hancock Insurance to start Portfolio Management Systems, a computer-based model that helped judge investment risk. He kept up this work even after enrolling at HBS and he grew the firm to 40 employees. He remembered, "I did lots of travel my first year and unfortunately skipped a lot of classes. I was probably on the bubble when they considered whether to invite me back for the second year."

Upon graduation, Lance sold his company to Fidelity Mutual Life and stayed on for a year as required by the sale. He then went back to Houston real estate, converting apartment rentals into condominiums worth $300 million over a ten-year period. After cashing out his real estate, he went looking for acquisitions. He bought a furniture company in Buffalo at a good price before he discovered "the books were cooked." It was a painful experience. After two years of legal battles and $2 million in costs, the furniture company was taken back by the sellers.

During this challenging period, Lance was above board in dealing with his financial backers, he said, and they were willing to fund another acquisition. This one was Mid-Continent Bottlers, with Lance receiving 15% of the deal for arranging the financing. The company had five bottling plants, one of which was losing money. He got management involved in the losing plant, turned it into a profitable operation, and sold it for $40 million. He then sold the other plants, in the process turning his $3 million stake into $65 million in less than 18 months.

With this major success behind him, he made several other acquisitions. Perhaps the most interesting was Larami Toys. He took a 60% interest in this company, whose key product was a battle-type squirt gun that soon was outlawed in California after a child was shot by a policeman while holding what looked like a real gun. This action in California stopped sales to the national toy chains. Lance redesigned the gun to make it more colorful and less real, and changed the name from "Drencher" to "Super-Soaker."

He then promoted the item with TV ads, in the process making it the most successful toy launch in history. Lance wound up selling the company to its management for three times what he had paid because he had given options to management that they exercised. This same management sold it for 20 times their purchase price two years later to Hasbro. Lance's creative genius profited him, but profited others even more.

In the early '90s, the banks that had required only 5% equity for acquisitions became more conservative and required 20–30% equity. Lance semi-retired and decided to participate in the Olympics.

He personally funded two bobsled teams for America Samoa since he could join them as an American. "I was the driver of one team," he proudly remembered. The team qualified for the competition in Norway, but just before the Olympics, Lance was beaten out for the lead driver position by a teammate, a Navy Seal of Samoan ancestry. Lance stepped aside and went to the Olympics as an alternate.

In 1994, Lance went back to the business world as a marketer of products using 1-800 numbers on television. He offered 20 products, including "8-minute abs" and "instant flower garden." He then took a step forward. He went to the cable TV companies and said he'd split profits 50-50 if they would give him their unsold commercial advertising time. They agreed and he made more money as an ad reseller. He then took the business even further. He would manage ad time for cable companies by buying large blocks of time and reselling it. Since cable companies sold mainly local ads, they all agreed. Lance then put together a national ad sale capability. He went to major national advertisers such as car companies and offered audience "views" for one-third the cost of traditional network television. From 1995 to 2008, his TelAmerica Media grew from zero to $100 million in revenues, and he sold most of the company for $85 million, retaining 15% ownership.

In looking back at his successes, Lance credited recognizing opportunities that others didn't, and being willing to go "all in" when he thought he was right. He continues to live life on his own schedule, which now includes 10 to 12 poker tournaments a year, as much golf as possible, and work as an active consultant to an education foundation that he and his wife Christina founded in 2008.

Making "Traks"

Another innovator who took an idea and changed an industry was Bill Danner, a Harvard undergrad who arrived at HBS with seven years of work experience, half at Proctor & Gamble and half with the U.S. Navy. Eager to start his own business after graduation, he and three classmates discovered a company in receivership being liquidated by its two Boston-lawyer owners. The company had been in the cross-country ski business and had been unsuccessful. Bill and his partners offered a royalty payment on skis sold with a small up-front cash payment and got a license to make a fish-scale pattern ski with a no-wax base. This new ski style made cross country skiing easier for the masses. As ease of use was combined with a growing fitness movement, sales took off. The new company became the well-recognized Trak Ski Company. Fifteen factories worldwide were established and annual revenues approached $25 million.

As the Trak company grew, it began to attract the attention of foreign governments (especially Austria, France, and Yugoslavia). These governments wanted to protect their domestic manufacturers of skis, and Trak was soon competing against firms that received heavy government subsidies. Recognizing that the business faced an uphill race rather than a smooth glide, Bill cashed in by selling to Olin, a large downhill ski maker. Bill then moved into consulting and established "Leisure Trends," a tracking service that helped identify and track new leisure themes.

In discussing entrepreneurship, Bill praised innovation but flatly stated, "If you think you have a totally new idea, it just means you've been lazy and haven't researched the internet enough." In other words, almost always someone else is doing or has done what you think is new. Bill advised not to be discouraged. "You have to find a need and articulate the need, and find the product that solves the need." Given his own experience, Bill offers two other bits of wisdom: "Look down the road and think how the competition will react and think in advance how to counter that. Also, surround yourself with people who will be better than you are, and be sure you enjoy the reflection from their success."

You Can't Miss Them All

Another perspective on startups comes from Richard Sheldon, one of perhaps a dozen grads of HBS's Class of 1970 who can best be described as serial entrepreneurs. After starting out with a traditional and secure job, he started questioning where he was going. At age 30, he ventured out on his own when a student in an MBA class he was teaching at the University of Connecticut suggested buying a 100-year-old bra and girdle company. The company was alive, but barely. Fortunately for Richard, in the early '90s, the sexy and form-fitting Spandex came on the scene. Sales quickly went from $12 million to $40 million. "Even a dead business can get lucky," he observed.

Next, he had an idea to put ads on paper towels with coupons inside the paper cylinders. After that, he got involved in making and selling pizza under the Ray's Pizza name, which was success-ful enough that he opened six more stores. A dispute with his part-ner led him to sell out. "Soda was the profit maker, not pizza," he remembered.

Soon, he was finding ideas and identifying people who could invest 8–20% of the money required, knew the industry, and were willing to put in a disproportionate share of the money relative to their net worth. These people became managers while Richard was the CEO and handled the finances and marketing. "I like the an-nuities that can come from successful small businesses."

He started over 20 companies, but none more interesting or controversial than a surrogate parenting business. This company helped males become sperm donors to women who would carry the baby and give up the baby after its birth. In the late '80s, he opened the Infertility Center of New York. Over the next five years for a fee of $8,000, he helped 800 childless couples get children. Eventually, surrogate parenting was banned in New York and 30 other states. He still gets thank-you cards from some parents, but he wasn't sorry the

94

business was shut down. "I didn't want a 75-year-old man going to a PTA meeting with his mistress," he said.

Richard continues to start businesses, pointing out that "entrepreneurial people don't retire at 65." His advice to those who want to follow his lead: "Keep swinging. You can't miss them all."

BIG MONEY FOR REAL ESTATE

Entrepreneur Peter Aldrich marched to a different drummer for much of his varied and successful career. Even at HBS he took a different path, serving as chairman of a controversial HBS Vietnam Peace Committee and running an anti-war petition drive at the start of his second year. At graduation, he initially taught at the school while pursuing a doctoral degree, but after one year, quit both and went into mortgage banking and real estate development. This effort collapsed with the real estate market in 1974, so he and his wife hopped on motorcycles and spent several months riding around eastern Canada.

In 1975, Peter pioneered the investment of institutional pension and endowment funds into real estate. He convinced the Boston Company to finance his efforts through a subsidiary of which he was president. This effort prospered, but a brokerage firm bought the Boston Company in 1981, so Peter left to co-found AEW Capital Management. This firm became one of the largest global real estate investment advisors, with an $18 billion property portfolio (now over $50 billion). In 1997, he retired as chairman and began buying international operating companies. He also started businesses and explored investments in places as diverse as the Soviet Union, Mexico, China, Vietnam, and Cuba.

A cancer scare caused a re-thinking of what he wanted to do, so in 2000 he became an art student and an angel investor, providing seed capital for startups and helping with international capital formation. "That sort of investing has done well. I learned that it's management that makes the difference, and a bad leader or manager can screw up a good product." He invested in a half dozen companies, and played a very active role in the now public Zip Car.

Peter readily acknowledges that luck has been very important to his business success. "The world belongs to those who recognize good luck and are prepared to take risks, especially when they're young. Prepare for the worst but be ready to take advantage of the good." He likes to quote Winston Churchill's observation: "Success is the ability to go from one failure to another with no loss of enthusiasm."

Peter spends a lot of time painting now, especially baseball scenes from Fenway Park. As one classmate described him: "Peter is retired and enjoys: time with his children; swimming; fly-fishing; baseball; motorcycling; oil painting and water coloring; ancient Greek pottery; golf; American painting; astronomy; model trains; and any good book, good company, or good friend."

FIND YOUR PASSION

Paul McLaughlin had earned a metallurgical engineering degree from Rensselaer and a master's in material science from Lehigh before coming to HBS. He was ready to join a startup company after graduation. Before he started, the company he was to join went belly-up. Luckily, a lecturer at Harvard who taught one of HBS's few new venture courses steered him to General Electric in Schenectady, where he joined the technological innovation group. He spent two years there and then GE made him president of a spin-off company and gave him an equity stake. Stints as general manager of a high purity metals company for the semiconductor industry, and a general manager spot for a firm making equipment for plasma systems, followed.

In 1996, Paul seized the chance to run his own show. With only $3.5 million in equity from an investment company and $50 million in debt, he engineered the acquisition of Rudolph Technologies, a high-tech company making capital equipment for the semiconductor industry that Paul took public in 1999. As CEO, he set to work strengthening Asian business where two-thirds of his sales were. His stock went from 33 cents to $50 per share, for a total market value of nearly $1 billion. The tech bubble burst in 2002 and the stock slid back to $9 a share. Paul continues to be active in the company and spends a lot of time traveling the world while overseeing Rudolph's 700 employees.

Thinking about his career, Paul said he did his best work when he was having fun. "Work at something that's your passion. If it doesn't fit or feel right, don't be afraid to move on."

OUT-CHINESE THE CHINESE

"You need to pick an expanding industry and get a competitive advantage." These words of advice came from Chris Stowell, a classmate who leveraged an ability to speak Russian, a Harvard MBA, a master's degree in international relations from Johns Hopkins, and a short-term political appointment to a company specializing in east-west trade before it became popular.

Chris worked with Commerce Secretary Maurice Stans, chairman of a newly created East-West Trade Committee, before starting his own firm in 1971. He had the vision to see that the Soviet Bloc and China, while then isolated from the mainstream of U.S. business activity, were not likely to remain that way. Initially, he served as a facilitator for U.S. companies seeking export opportunities with the U.S.S.R. and Eastern Europe. He quickly learned that Russians will bluff when negotiating deals, but when they sign a contract, they honor it.

In 1973, he expanded to China, where he found people easy to talk with but not as likely to honor a contract as they would a favorable relationship. He learned to compliment the Chinese freely while making sure to maintain a humble bearing himself. Chris used the phrase "out-Chinese the Chinese," meaning to respond to their praise by giving back even greater praise. Deals to make things in China followed, and he expanded to doing deals himself. He started three companies, each with a good Chinese partner that he described as critical to ultimate success. He sold all three for a profit. By 1985, he had become totally oriented to China, with 58 people employed there by his firm. The economy turned down and by 1987, he had only 14 employees. He learned the wisdom of not over-extending his reach.

More recently, Chris has started SDP Energy, a power distribution business for green energy. He perfected the process of cogeneration in China, using natural gas to power small utility plants and recovering the heat from the engine and exhaust heat exchanger. He has expanded this business to the United States where he is helping hotels produce both heat and electricity using natural gas to save 40% on their bills and reduce CO_2 emissions. "You have to be a bulldog, take the punches, and hang on to that 'leg' until you win, but I love the challenges of a startup," he said.

INSURING NEW GRADS

Following graduation, Mike Collins returned to Texas to earn a living, first at a high-tech company but later at Fidelity Union Life Insurance in Dallas. Fidelity had been founded by his grandfather in the '20s and Mike joined as assistant to the president. He was made president in 1973 and continued until 1982, riding the roller coaster of Texas-sized booms and busts that caused the firm's borrowers to collapse and left Fidelity owning many small regional malls in the southwest. Michael worked to improve occupancy. He also expanded the life insurance business to all 50 states by recruiting 2,000 new agents and focusing on insuring recent college graduates. His success prompted the large German financial company Allianz to buy Fidelity. Michael became president of Allianz Investment Corporation, reporting to the CEO in Munich.

In 1983, Michael decided to make his own way, starting a telecommunications business and moving on to real estate, ranching, timber, and oil and gas. He also opened a small hedge fund to concentrate on shorting stocks that he felt were fraudulent. He picked a bad time to short as the stock market went straight up and, he said, "Most of my friends thought I was crazy." He was 95% net short from 1983 to 1987 and 100% short on Black Monday in 1987 when the market crashed. He managed to achieve a 68% annualized rate of return from 1983 to 1987. In late 1987, he merged his hedge fund with a West Coast firm and took his money out.

By 1994, he had started Collins Capital, a Fund of Funds using 80 managers to invest the money. It now has a billion dollars under management and from 1994 to 2008, when, he said, "all the liquidity went out of the market," his compounded returns were 15% annually.

Michael now lives in Florida, with a second home in Dallas. He travels 200,000 miles a year on American Airlines alone, and is on the board of the Smithsonian, is chairman of the board at the Institute of Contemporary Art, Miami, and chairman of the executive committee of the Friends of Florence, an organization he co-founded to help restore art treasures in that Italian city. As for investing, he advised to "cut your losses." He tries to mentor and help others in the business, but thinks, "Most have to learn their lessons by experiencing mistakes by themselves."

APPLYING TECHNOLOGY

Tim Davis calls it a mistake that he went right from college to HBS. He took a year off in between the two years of his MBA program to gain some real-world experience in banking, returning to graduate in 1971, although he counts himself as part of the Class of 1970.

His parents had been involved in entrepreneurial activities, and he did the same. He returned to his native Vermont and started a sports adventure company, then opened a woolen hat and sweater clothing company, a real estate operation, and a maple syrup business.

After four years in Vermont, he moved to San Francisco to open a data-based firm that published various directories. He sold the business in 1983 and returned to Vermont and over the next 25 years, started half a dozen companies, all oriented to using advanced materials in areas such as fiber optics, electronics, semiconductors, and coatings technologies.

Tim's main thrust was finding what he described as "an application of technology that people didn't know they needed, but loved once they saw it." Surprisingly, in building these companies he found that people were more important than the technology in making a firm a success. One of these startups began at about $500,000 per year in revenues and was sold at three times revenue when it reached $1 million per month.

Tim now uses his successful experiences to run a small venture capital company, Fresh Tracks Capital, from his Vermont home. He reviews hundreds of business plans. He hopes his winners will return ten times his investment in three to five years. He almost always begins as a minority investor but takes control if more funds are needed. He estimates that his failures were not because the people were bad, but because they were wrong for the positions they held. He estimates that about half of his startups need a change in CEO as they move forward.

A BAD EMPLOYEE

"I'm not a good employee," said Carl Novotny as he explained why he decided to pursue an entrepreneurial career in financial services marketing. Carl wrote a paper while at HBS on the venture capital industry, and remained there for an extra year to further explore the industry and to write case studies for the school. His first startup didn't work out, so he took a job as CFO for a company arranging speakers for events. He moved on to join Trans National Travel, which at the time was marketing affinity travel. The effort was redefined as affinity group marketing, and in 1982, he tried to offer credit cards through groups. Banks at the time were marketing credit cards only locally.

He decided to approach this credit card effort with an ally, Maryland National Bank. Together, they enlisted five other banks so the cards could be offered nationally. The third group to sign up was the American Dental Association. When 28% of its members responded to a test-marketing card solicitation, Carl knew they were on to something. In the next 18 months, they enrolled 400 other groups. Carl became COO and wisely accepted a lower salary and a bigger piece of the ownership. After five years, Carl was fired over a dispute on how his bonus should be awarded. At age 41, he had to litigate to get the 20% of company shares that he had earned. When he won the lawsuit, he was rich, but was forced to sign a five-year non-compete agreement. Five years later, he started competing, owning 50% of First USA Partners. That firm did 3,000 affinity group sales and was doing $40 million in annual revenue when Bank One bought the company in 1997.

With money in his pockets, Carl started the Venture Capital Fund of New England. Since 2001, he has invested in 27 different situations. As for spending his money, he said, "I've spent more on others than I have on myself." He encourages young people to start something for themselves. He observed, "Young people don't know what they don't know, so they have that as an advantage. They don't know all the obstacles. They just go and do it."

A LITTLE OF THIS, A LITTLE OF THAT

Graduates of Harvard Business School like to think they can run any business, regardless of type. Stan Barnes's diverse career proved that at least some, like Stan, are willing to try. After four years in the Navy and two years at HBS, Stan took a job at King Broadcasting in Seattle, doing research initially but soon acting as the general manager of a classical music radio station that he turned from losing money to profitable in four years.

The following three years, Stan ran a furniture factory. Nothing unusual except the factory was intended to provide paying jobs for ex-cons, and was sponsored by the U.S. Dept. of Labor and the Ford Foundation. The company had 15 workers with traditional skills teamed with 85 employees who had been criminals, drug users, etc. Stan was president and had a goal to place people in unsubsidized jobs. Funding for the furniture factory went away, so Stan moved the group to working as subassembly people for Boeing.

Buying a recreational boat business followed, but an oil embargo and high gas prices killed the company and persuaded Stan better opportunities could be had in growing big, consistent, non-seasonal businesses. Nearly 15 years as an independent consultant followed. He led a name change campaign for Westin Hotels, did marketing and business planning for turnaround situations, helped start a radio station, assisted several small companies in raising capital, and even worked on a soy business in Russia.

In 2005, he became an "algae entrepreneur," developing a biofuel more energy-efficient than corn ethanol. He located his processing equipment near large dairy farms where he used cow manure to grow algae in large water tanks well-exposed to sunlight. This was then turned into fuel, especially for the aviation industry. Boeing was a backer of the project, which is ongoing.

In reviewing his career, Stan said, "Success is inside oneself, not 'out there'." He asked proudly, "How many people have benefitted from what I've done?" The important things to have are persistence and self-awareness. "Figure out what you're good at," he advised.

SKIPPING COLLEGE

An early introduction into what is required of a successful entrepreneur helped mark the path for Donn Fletcher, one of the very few who earned an MBA from HBS but has no college degree. Donn's dad helped him get started at age ten by having him run a drive-in grocery store. He quickly learned to do the math calculations required in his head. In 1955, at age 15, he was making $500 per week at the store. He did well in high school and was planning on becoming an architect. His plans changed, however, when he got his girlfriend pregnant, married her, and dropped out of school. He took a job at age 19 as a $60 per week laborer.

Donn moved up in the construction business, running a back hoe while doing rough architectural drawings on the side to earn extra money. When a nuclear scare swept the United States in the late '50s, he designed fallout shelters and sold them. He left Texas for California to handle sales for a company building rigid steel structures. In 1963, he was drafted by the U.S. Army and trained for jungle warfare. He then went on to every military program he could get into, including Ranger School where he was made a sergeant and asked to train others. He was in advanced infantry training when he was assigned the task of remodeling a hospital with a 24-man team. He also took, and passed, the office candidate test, was commissioned, and joined the Army's Corp of Engineers, the only draftee and non-college grad in it. In 1965, he left the Army and worked for three years with his father putting up buildings until they had a falling-out. A personal interview with HBS Professor Tony Athos got him an unlikely acceptance into HBS.

He worked a summer job between HBS years for Pier 1 Imports, which was rumored to include CIA operatives in its organization, and was hired after graduation. He was told to spend a year working in a store and spend an equal amount of time in a warehouse. When he balked at this assignment, he was told to report to the CEO, who told him to visit every store and write a report on what was being done right and wrong. He traveled widely, including Australia for 18 months and then Europe. After three years, he was made chief operating officer for this New York Stock Exchange firm. Between 1974 and 1978, he helped double sales, even though poor-performing stores were being closed. After this the CEO, who Donn believed was fearful of competition for his own job, hired a consultant. Donn thought the consultant was given instructions to prepare a negative report on his performance. Donn took the hint and quit Pier 1.

His next job was with a smaller store chain in California that sold linens and garden tools. It was losing money, so he got rid of a warehouse and direct-shipped merchandise to stores. In three years, it was profitable and profit margins had risen from 20% to 35%. In 1985, he got a call from an executive recruiter who invited him to join 20th Century Fox as an executive. He stayed for five years, helping make the movie studio profitable. While there, he arranged to use the tall building setting for the film "Die Hard."

Donn said he personally has "a low tolerance for crap," and doesn't believe he needed a Harvard degree to be successful. In fact, he believes he would have made more money by taking business risks on his own if he hadn't gone to HBS. He admitted, however, he wouldn't have had as much fun.

A GOOD WIFE AND A GOOD LIFE

Spending half his business career preparing to run his own company helped make the second half a success for Jim Latimer, now running his own oil company in Texas. Jim had been in the Army's ROTC program, but was granted a 53-week delay in entering the Army when he graduated from HBS. He used the opportunity to work as an auditor for the accounting firm Coopers & Lybrand in New York, gaining the minimum year of experience before taking the Certified Public Accounting (CPA) exam, which he passed. In June, 1971, the Army sent him not to Vietnam but to Washington, where he joined classmate Hank Paulson working for Secretary of Defense Melvin Laird. He spent two years evaluating weapon systems for possible acquisition.

After the service, he went back to Boston, where his wife began to earn her own MBA from HBS while he did consulting for utilities and energy firms. Among his assignments was spending six months in Washington advising on the Arab oil embargo of 1973. In 1976, he joined the New York office of the consulting firm McKinsey & Co. His clients were chemical companies and energy companies. When the second oil embargo of 1981 raised oil prices again, he moved to Texas and joined an operating oil company and did oil field engineering and consulting as a sideline. In 1987, he became co-head of the Dallas office of Prudential Insurance, which at the time was investing more than a billion dollars a year in the oil business. He stayed for five years.

In 1992, Jim was ready to run his own oil company, using 3-D seismic studies to locate oil for various joint venture and partnership investors. He also worked as a court-appointed turnaround expert, assigned to help reorganize eight different troubled oil firms. "It was something I was reasonably good at doing," he said. In 2004, he took on his toughest challenge, joining the board of the infamous Enron Corporation after its problems forced it to submit a reorganization plan to the bankruptcy court. The board, and Jim, worked for six years to straighten out the mess, and managed payouts to creditors that were three times the initial expectations.

Jim is amazed at the extraordinary technological progress that has been made over the past 15 years in the oil and gas business. He's also amazed that the public awareness of all this progress has been low or nonexistent. "Our ability to identify sources of oil and extract it is remarkable," he said. As for handling business decisions in general, he advised employees to "learn to live with instability."

Circumstances change, whether you try to stay on the right path or not. He advised, try to be "the person who knows what they're doing, not the person who's been there forever. Tenure should not be relied on." He also emphasized that in moving forward in a business career, "the most important thing to have is a good wife."

GONE FISHING

Working as a consultant with the Arthur D. Little firm in Boston was the starting point after graduation for Charlton Ames. He stayed for five years, including one year in Brazil advising the generals who ran the national steel company on the issues of personnel, governance, and marketing. Although he enjoyed consulting, this descendant of the oldest corporation in the United States (Ames Shovel, founded in 1774) was more interested in startups and small businesses. In 1978, he founded Ames and Wellman, a venture capital operation providing debt financing to small companies in Maine. "The institutional venture capitalists didn't come to Maine because the deals were too small," he commented.

He did this for a while and then raised money for a new equity venture pool. He put the money to work with businesses in Maine. As he expected, there were no big winners or losers in the portfolio. He had successes, but not big successes. After nearly 17 years, he decided it was time to close the operation down. "I'm proud that we were able to wind it up cleanly and pay off investors," he said.

In 1990, he ventured into deeper waters by starting Sea Run Holdings, an aquaculture business in Casco Bay, Maine. The idea was to raise salmon in a hatchery and release them into the ocean, harvesting them when they grew bigger and returned. If only 2% of the salmon returned, the operation would be economical. Unfortunately, when the Alaskan salmon fisheries realized they were creating a competitor, the salmon egg shipments ceased and so did the operation.

106

About this time, Charlton met a biotech researcher, Evelyn Sawyer, who suggested factoring proteins out of salmon blood. "It was a brilliant value-added business," he said, using salmon from nearby farming operations and selling the blood plasma as reagents for laboratory diagnostic work. They also found that the matrix patches that could be built might help in wound healing and stop traumatic bleeding. Although no human testing had been done, the Defense Department showed an interest in how matrix patches might be used with vascular grafts.

As Charlton guides his company into the future, he admits to adopting a pragmatic approach. "We have to pay attention to cash flow or we could get into serious trouble. We need a partner who has a practical product."

6

SUCCESS AS AN ENTREPRENEUR

B EFORE 1970, HBS PROVIDED LITTLE training in the art and science of starting and growing a business, but it did accept people who showed intelligence, flexibility, and the ability to get things done. These attributes are ideal for startups. With job loyalty in the corporate world beginning to fade, many 1970 HBS graduates in the '80s found another path to make a living. They gave up a regular paycheck and bet on their own talents to be successful as entrepreneurs.

In some cases, starting anew was something forced upon the person receiving a pink slip from a company. More often, however, a conscious decision was made to forego a generous paycheck for a possibly bigger eventual financial reward and the personal satisfaction of being your own boss. Each individual who achieved success did so in his own unique way, but some common threads are apparent.

The first is to identify a need before others and try to fill it. This requires spotting trends early and picking an expanding industry where you can get and hold a competitive advantage. The product or services do not have to be unique, but a person needs to know what advantages he has to get and retain customers. The biggest threat to a startup is running out of cash, so it's best to begin cautiously until the business is generating revenue (but not necessarily profits). Once a company has revenue, it can move to establish a positive cash flow by expanding product sales to new outlets and attract investment capital. Even the best idea can require adjustments during the launch stage, and by running out of capital you also run out of time to adjust.

Young entrepreneurs are the heroes of today's business world. The reason for this may be that the young have less to lose when they take on risks, and they don't worry about obstacles until they actually encounter them. They don't know what they don't know so, as Nike says, they "just do it." Lawyers are widely thought to make poor entrepreneurs, perhaps because their training is to anticipate and avoid problems, and therefore they aren't willing to take the risks of a startup.

A good idea is to start a business you can be passionate about. The long hours seem less of a burden if you enjoy what you're doing. Also try to figure out what you're good at and anticipate the eventual question: How many people have benefitted from what I've done? If you think you have a new idea, it's probably because you haven't conducted adequate research to find who is already in the market as a competitor. Don't be surprised if you start something and later learn somebody else is already making or doing it and that company is ahead of yours.

Remember that management, not the product, makes the difference. The product will evolve as you progress. Prepare a business plan, but be ready to abandon it as you gather more information. Surround yourself with people who are better at what they do than you. Empower your employees to make decisions and trust those decisions. Nothing builds support like asking people what they think.

There will be booms and busts in the economy, so don't over-extend your reach. If appropriate, get local partners to work with you if they can supply contacts and knowledge that you don't have.

To be a successful entrepreneur, you have to be a bulldog and be ready to absorb the punches a startup throws at you. Learn to live with instability and adjust as circumstances change. Be honest with your investors and treat them fairly. If the business is successful and grows to a significant size, don't be surprised if others believe a new CEO should be brought in to run the business. Building a company and managing it generally require different skills. If you can achieve success and find other capable people to run what you started and accept an advisory role, you've achieved personal freedom seldom found in the corporate world. But remember—entrepreneurial people rarely retire at 65.

7

BUILDING A BUSINESS

I F YOU ASK WHAT WORD first comes to mind when someone is described as a graduate of Harvard Business School, the answer
is likely to be "rich." Often that's true, but certainly not every
graduate falls into the millionaire-or-higher category. There are,
however, at least three members (and probably more) of the Class of
1970 who have achieved billionaire status. In the chapter, "Winning
on Wall Street," Canadian Gerry Schwartz is mentioned. He's the
founder and CEO of Onex, Canada's largest private equity firm. As
of March 2015, Forbes estimated his fortune at $1.71 billion. Gerry
was proud to discuss his successes. Not all classmates felt the same.

PRESS-SHY INVESTORS
Among classmates reluctant to talk were Joe Steinberg and Ian Cum-
mings. They took control of what became Leucadia National Corporation in January 1979 and stepped down from active management
in March of 2013. During those 34 years, the two of them built a
major holding company with subsidiaries involved in mining and

drilling, telecommunications, healthcare, manufacturing, banking and lending, insurance, brokerage, real estate, and wineries. The NYSE-traded company's stock price compounded at better than 25% annually. By March of 2008, Forbes listed Joe (then 64) as worth $1.5 billion (#785 on the World's Billionaires list) and Ian (then age 67) as worth $1.3 billion (#897). Joe and some classmates got an early start in business while still in school by attempting to redevelop Boston's waterfront. This major effort went nowhere in the melting pot of Boston politics, but it did demonstrate that Joe was not one to shy away from a challenge. A similar approach was evident when he tried to get a job from the New York City merchant banking firm Karl Marx. He was turned down but, according to an HBS classmate, he showed up and started working anyway.

Ian did not respond to a request for an interview. Joe refused a request with the comment that he didn't believe he had any special insights to offer people pursuing business careers. Fortunately, these press-shy value investors were very open in their annual letters to shareholders, which were very much like Warren Buffet's Berkshire Hathaway shareholder letters: folksy and to the point. In fact, Leucadia and Berkshire Hathaway formed a 50-50 joint venture in 2009 ("Berkadia") to acquire the largest non-bank provider of commercial mortgage servicing (handling $240 billion of commercial mortgage loans) utilizing a back office processing center in India.

The 1992 report explained Leucadia's general acquisition approach: "We search for niches, not dominance, on the theory that the world can tolerate many mice but few elephants." The wisdom of this strategy was apparent when the company bought Colonial Penn Life and Colonial Penn Casualty for $128 million. The acquisition had a portfolio of scary insurance risks, but these were dealt with in the next six years, with Leucadia receiving $300 million in management fees, dividends, and tax-sharing payments. Both of these acquired firms were then sold for a total of $1.5 billion.

The 2000 Leucadia annual report states, however, that "other insurance company purchases were not as successful."

Another insight into Leucadia's style was discussed in the 2002 annual report: "We follow our own few rules. First, don't overpay. Second, don't overstate earnings or the balance sheet. Third, pay as little tax as the law allows. Fourth, don't break the rules. Following these principles has led to satisfactory growth in shareholders' equity and peace of mind."

A further elaboration on strategy was explained in 2006's report: "We tend to be buyers of assets and companies that are troubled or out of favor and as a result are selling substantially below the values which we believe are there.... We are not income statement driven." They also were cautious on the international front: "We have a well-founded skepticism towards investments in places where the rule of law is not well-developed."

Along with more traditional business purchases, the company made a $95 million purchase of vineyards in Napa Valley, California, and Willamette Valley, Oregon. Leucadia shareholders can buy wines at a 20% discount, but there were also personal incentives. Ian and Joe admitted in their 2009 newsletter that "we are both getting long in the tooth." They defended the wine purchase by writing, "We remind you that wine is food and it fosters both good times and laughter with family and friends. In these times, we all need as much of that as we can get." Ian has hosted several events at the vineyards for his Section C classmates.

ONE WAY TO RUN A RAILROAD

Not content with just a law degree, Mort Fuller decided to get a business degree from Harvard. He arrived on campus in 1968 and soon connected with three section mates who shared an interest in entrepreneurial adventures. One of the three was Joe Steinberg, mentioned above for the growth of Leucadia. In 1969, they pitched an idea to the Boston Redevelopment Authority to remodel the old City Hall in Boston. "At the time," Mort remembered, "we had no sense that this would be an impossible task." They failed in their efforts, despite legal representation by eventual presidential candidate Michael Dukakis. The challenge, however, was a great experience. They moved on and bought an island off the Maine coast and established a granite quarry. They made a little money by syndicating it to investors. For Mort, a stint with a real estate firm in Ohio followed, but he left when his request for an equity piece earned the response, "We're a family business, and you're not family."

He found his niche by joining a small railroad in upstate New York called Genesee and Wyoming (G&W), then with only 14 miles of track transporting road salt for its only customer. The job shift wasn't as strange as it first appears, since Mort's great grandfather had bought the railroad in 1899 and Mort had joined the board in 1973. Mort then bought a big block of stock from a charity and, with his father's stock, had over 50% ownership. He became CEO in 1977 when G&W became a holding company with 50 employees.

The business saw opportunity to grow after 1980 when railroads became less regulated. Previously, any railroad looking to terminate employees had to give the person terminated six years of wages and benefits. The new law didn't require this. Mort contacted big railroads and industrial companies with their own railroad operations and started acquiring pieces no longer needed or wanted. He also offered to be the contract railroad operator for others. By using a disciplined approach to transactions, he was able to finance sensible acquisition growth, allowing him to acquire his bigger competitors. He eventually made 34 acquisitions and built Genesee and Wyoming into a railroad with over 10,000 miles of track operating in 26 U.S. states, Canada, Australia, and the Netherlands.

In 2009, after going public in 1996 and listing first on Nasdaq and then the New York Stock Exchange, the company had $600 million in revenues and 2,400 employees. G&W subsequently lost about 2,500 miles of track in Australia when that operation was sold in 2007, but more than recovered by acquiring its largest competitor (Rail America) in 2012. With this last transaction, G&W had 15,000 miles of track, 111 different railroad operations, 4,600 employees, $1.5 billion in pro forma revenue, and a $5 billion market value. Revenues were split 70% in the United States, 20% in Australia, and 10% in Canada, with a small revenue stream in the Netherlands and Belgium.

Mort credits having early control of the company with letting him pursue his vision. He also recruited directors he trusted who would give him advice. He relied on his super voting shares (ten times the vote of the ordinary shares) to keep the company independent when, in 1999, it was trading at only four times next year's projected earnings. He also took advantage of the depressed share price by having the company buy back 25% of the shares outstanding at the time. He was aggressive with his acquisitions but never assumed he had to do any particular deal. He also "left my ego at the door," he said, and looked to hire people who would do the same.

SUCCESS IN REAL ESTATE

Real estate was a hot commodity in the late '60s, so it's not surprising that a number of classmates entered the business in 1970. Included in this group were three section mates (Section B) who took their first-year classes together but followed separate and very successful paths into real estate. Although the three were interviewed independently, they all emphasized the need for integrity and strong ethical values to succeed. They also felt a strong desire to give something back to the communities that helped them prosper.

Bill White said he was only a mediocre student at Lehigh University, majoring in mathematics and graduating in 1963 with a 2.4 GPA average. He enlisted in the Navy's officer candidate school and was subsequently accepted into Navy SEAL training. Only 18 of his 140-person training class finished the program. Bill served on Underwater Demolition and SEAL teams for the Navy for nearly five years before beginning HBS. Upon graduation, he moved from Boston to San Francisco and worked for four years at a real estate management and development firm. He was made president, but when fired 30 days later, he decided it was time to start his own firm. Through building development and acquisitions over the next 20 years and the use of private equity, he subsequently grew the firm to 55 employees and 2½ million square feet of office and other commercial space.

Bill's son has been running the firm for some time now and has significantly expanded the scope and size of the business. Bill and his wife have found time to open a small hotel in southern France where they vacation as guests. His advice for those working in real estate was to "put the people who invest with you first, even if it's to your disadvantage." He also recommended hiring smart and caring people that you pay well but demand a lot of. He stressed maintaining one's integrity, no matter how difficult, and showing respect for employees. He personally spends 30% of his time working with nonprofit groups, including the Navy SEAL Foundation. He also goes to church and practices his religious faith regularly.

John "Chip" Akridge also began in commercial real estate upon graduation, first with an established firm. In 1974, he moved out on his own with startup capital provided by Carl Marks and Company (a New York City merchant bank) at the urging of classmate Joe Steinberg, who initially worked there before he became president of the successful NYSE firm Leucadia. Working in the D.C. metropolitan area, Chip built or acquired 12 million square feet of properties, 90% in office buildings with 80% located in D.C. His company employed 185 people, half working in the office and half in the field. Chip adopted a conservative approach to the cyclical business. In each of his projects he chose a partner, usually a large institution that could be called on if financing became difficult.

This strategy saved him when others leveraged with real estate ran out of money in tough times.

In 1990, Chip's firm won an international award for the best office building renovation. He also received an award for one of the top 50 buildings built in the world, at 1201 New York Ave. in D.C., with a building designed by I.M. Pei. In both buildings, a key reason for the honors was incorporating sustainability features such as energy conservation. He also has regularly been recognized as having the best property management service in his size category.

Chip's current efforts are heavily directed towards fundraising for the Trust for the National Mall, an organization which he serves as chairman. He noted that the D.C. National Mall has 700 acres with 30 million visitors, more than the Grand Canyon, Yosemite, and Yellowstone combined. Unfortunately, for years the under-funded Park Service has deferred maintenance on the Mall, and it shows.

In looking back at his rewarding career, Chip credited "having strong values—legal, moral and ethical." He added, "I thank God every day for the success I've had."

Unlike Bill and Chip, Don King didn't establish his own real estate firm. Instead, he spent his first six years in San Francisco developing and financing apartment buildings and shopping centers, working with smaller firms. In 1974, when a serious credit crunch occurred and the ERISA (Employee Retirement Income Security Act) legislation was enacted, prompting minimum standards for pension investments, it seemed a good time to begin using pension fund capital to finance commercial real estate. He initiated such programs at Bank of America and Crocker National Bank.

In 1979, the fledgling investment advisor RREEF lured him to Chicago. For the next 25 years, he guided RREEF as its managing partner. RREEF became a fully integrated investment advisory firm providing opportunities in both the public and private markets. It handled separate accounts as well as investment funds across the full risk spectrum. In 1998, RREEF was sold to a Dutch company and subsequently to Deutsche Bank. Don was appointed global head of Deutsche Asset Management and then vice chairman before retiring in 2007.

Don now spends his time as he likes, teaching a real estate investment course at the University of Virginia during the colder months and fly fishing and bow hunting in Montana from mid-June to October. A University of Virginia alumnus, he is honored to be the chairman of the Thomas Jefferson Foundation, which owns and operates the historic landmark Monticello, once Thomas Jefferson's home in Charlottesville.

"I've seen a lot of cycles and was fortunate to miss the 2008–2009 debacle," Don noted. He was also thankful for a willingness to take unpopular positions. In 1987, RREEF began to realize there was a bubble building in certain office and industrial markets. He had the firm write down its portfolio values and sell a substantial number of assets, actions that were very unpopular with clients. After answering tough questions for the next two years, Don watched the entire real estate market collapse in 1990. RREEF was vindicated in both its views and actions. As the '90s progressed, RREEF was rewarded with client loyalty and major growth while others in real estate were busy sorting out their problems.

AN ORDINARY SEAMAN

If you're planning to start a business, it's a good idea to have some first-hand experience to help you make it a success. In the case of Ed Schneider, five summers serving as an ordinary seaman on a merchant ship was a great introduction to the container shipping business. Ed started with summer work at age 16, working eight hours a day on various cargo ships. By the time he was 21, he had already logged 1½ years at sea.

When Ed received his MBA, he was hired by Marine Midland Bank, impressing the interviewer who ran the national and

120

international lending areas of the bank enough to be hired as his assistant. He did this for a few years before moving to the southern United States as a commercial lender. In 1975, he joined Itel, a San Francisco company that invented the concept of leveraged leasing for equipment. In Ed's case, he focused on container leasing, working his way up to become director of finance.

In 1980, he and two others started Triton Container, each contributing $30,000 in equity and then borrowing a total of $50,000 more. This amount was clearly inadequate, so Ed met with the Pritzer family to seek further funding. The Pritzer family bought equity and launched limited partnerships to finance the containers purchased. The business prospered until 1986, when the tax code was changed to eliminate the investor tax credits so attractive to the limited partnerships doing the financing. Despite this tax change and a downturn in the shipping business, Triton used $7 million in retained earnings along with $15 million provided from preferred stock bought by the Pritzers and $10 million in insurance company debt to begin growing again.

By 2012, Triton owned $5 billion in shipping containers, the equivalent of 2.7 million container units, each 20 feet in length. It was the largest owned fleet available for lease. The company invested heavily in computer systems and had fewer than 200 employees at 20 offices around the world. At meetings there might be 20 different first languages, but everybody also spoke English. In 2010, the company was sold to the private equity firm of Warburg Pincus because the Pritzer family wanted to sell its shares. Ed agreed to stay on for a few years, and continues to do so, but admitted he won't miss the 6:15 a.m. to 6:15 p.m. workdays.

A HEALTHY BIG, BIG BUSINESS

Among all the members of Harvard Business School's graduating class of 1970, soft-spoken but hard-driving Bob Walter was the most successful builder of a major company. Bob borrowed $1.3 million to buy the ailing food distribution division of Consolidated Foods for $1.5 million in 1971. Initially called Cardinal Foods, he used acquisitions to grow the business and then pivot its direction, changing the name first to Cardinal Distribution and then to Cardinal Health. The company is now an over $100 billion revenue healthcare services company that he said is improving the cost-effectiveness of healthcare.

A Columbus, Ohio, native and a mechanical engineering graduate of Ohio University, he first learned at Rockwell International what he didn't want to do: work for a large, bureaucratic company that handled cost-plus government contracts that he said negated the need for efficiency, and where seniority was more important than ingenuity. He remained just six months before heading for HBS.

Upon graduation, he returned to Columbus to join a small investment firm. His instructions were to find a company to buy. He targeted Consolidated Foods' distribution division, but after negotiating the $1.5 million price, he discovered the investment firm didn't have the financial capital to complete the deal. The partners also weren't prepared to come up with cash. Bob scrambled and got the money needed with bank and SBIC (Small Business Investment Company) help, contributing himself and getting others to join in providing the $200,000 total equity needed. He admits to doing an incomplete job in screening the investment firm before signing on. Nevertheless, he took on the challenge of running the purchased division.

After four years, his investment partners wanted to cash out despite some progress in turning around the troubled business. Bob personally stepped up and bought out most of the others. He then owned 50% and the SBIC had 40%. He had confidence the problems could be solved, but knew more time was needed. In 1981, ten years after the initial purchase, Bob found an opportunity to buy a drug wholesaler. He recognized that in food distribution there were a few large competitors. However, in the drug and medical distribution business, competition was primarily among smaller firms. Bob knew he needed to change direction. When the SBIC objected to the acquisition and pushed to be bought out, he got more financing to make it happen. He solved his capital problem by going public 18 months later. At the stock offering price at the time of the initial public offering, the SBIC would have received 30 times what it actually was paid for the shares earlier. Bob viewed that mistake as what often happens when investors get impatient for a return and don't allow enough time for a business to succeed.

From 1980 to 1995, the company focused on buying pharmaceutical distribution businesses across the U.S. With strategy tightly focused on making pharmaceutical acquisitions, the market value of the company went from $27 million upon going public in 1983 to over $29 billion by the late 1990s. This happened despite selling the food business in 1987.

By 1995, Cardinal Health had national pharmaceutical distribution coverage with the scale and efficiency that size provided. "We were a middleman," said Bob, serving both the manufacturers of pharmaceuticals and the dispensers of prescriptions (retail stores, hospitals, clinics, doctors, etc.). At that point, he saw his new mission as enhancing relationships by offering more services. He bought Pyxis, a firm with an 82% market share that helped automate the distribution of prescriptions and medical products on the floors of hospitals. He bought Allegiance, the nation's leading manufacturer and distributor of medical, surgical, and laboratory products and services to hospitals. He bought a specialty packaging firm to better serve medical manufacturers. He took Cardinal into the manufacturing of disposables, and expanded sales to a worldwide market. He even had the company offer consulting services to medical suppliers and customers. Not every deal worked out, but most were successful because Cardinal only acquired strategic businesses that made Cardinal better able to serve its customers on both sides of the middleman position.

By 2001, Cardinal had increased its earnings by more than 20% annually for 15 consecutive years. By 2004, it was the third largest healthcare service provider in the United States with a market capitalization of over $40 billion and 50,000-plus employees, 40% outside the United States. In a 2003 issue of *Fortune* magazine, legendary investment advisor Peter Lynch of Fidelity Investments called Bob "one of the best managers I've ever seen." Confidence in Bob's leadership prompted the various Fidelity funds to own at one point over 15% of Cardinal's stock in aggregate. For fiscal year 2016 (ending 6/30/16), revenues were over $121 billion and operating earnings were $2.5 billion.

A major bump in the road that slowed Bob's success was an antitrust suit brought by the Federal Trade Commission when Cardinal attempted in 1998 to acquire Bergen Brunswig, a competing health supplies distributor. Bob fought to complete the deal, but eventually abandoned the effort. "The government has a lot more money than any company does, and doesn't have to move quickly," he explained. He later was involved in an SEC investigation about Cardinal's accounting practices. Cardinal was absolved of any possible improper accounting issues, but Bob had to delay his retirement for two years (to 2009) so he could deal with the SEC.

Now Bob, with his three sons, runs Talisman Capital Partners, a private equity firm funded by his family. The philosophy of the family is, according to Bob, "If you bring a business in, you're the one responsible for it." He also works as a director for three public companies: Nordstrom, American Express (as lead independent director), and Yum Brands (where he serves as non-executive chairman). Despite his busy workload, his golf handicap is only five. The week before this interview he shot his age, carding a 71 for 18 holes.

8

BUILDING FOR THE LONG TERM

I F YOU START A BUSINESS or buy one that proves successful enough
to expand, most individuals would move towards further growth.
This can be done with the intent to sell when it reaches an acceptable valuation. As an alternative, the company can also be grown
with the intent for it to last many years beyond the individual's involvement. Each of these objectives involves a different strategy,
especially when large financings are involved. Relinquish too much
equity too soon, and somebody else might take charge once you
have identified the path to success.

The HBS graduates in the previous chapter were building
something that would last. Financings were arranged with partners
often taken on to cushion potential damage in cyclical downturns,
especially in real estate. One individual identified pension funds as
sources for long-term money needed in commercial real estate projects. Another chose insurance companies that would provide initial
funds and, once a partner, would be a likely source of further cash

if it was needed. A container leasing firm arranged equity funding from a wealthy family to expand rapidly with the help of investment partnerships.

Going public on the stock market is a common way for a company to fund expansion plans, but the timing needs to be right or control of the company might be lost to others.

Cardinal Health grew to be great with public money, but not until founder Bob Walter had spent more than ten years guiding his firm's direction while buying out various partners who had different plans along the way. Likewise, railroad leader Mort Fuller took over as CEO and majority owner of Genesee and Wyoming in 1977, but didn't go public until 1996. In the interim years, he took advantage of government legal changes on how terminated employees needed to be compensated to reduce employment while at the same time growing through acquisitions. In cases where companies owned their own in-house railroad lines but didn't choose to sell, he stepped in as a contract operator. When he did take the company public, he maintained control with super majority shares for himself that may have kept the company from being acquired three years later when the stock dropped to only four times earnings.

Treating investors fairly is a key to maintaining access to capital. So is demonstrating integrity and strong ethical values in all business dealings. There are inevitable downturns as companies grow, and having financial support when things aren't going well preserves opportunities for the future.

9

HANDLING ADVERSITY

M ANY PEOPLE THINK THAT HBS graduates have smooth paths ahead of them as they embark upon a career. That is certainly not the case for many graduates. Life has a way of throwing curves like even the best of baseball pitchers. Those who aren't prepared strike-out and move to the sidelines. Fortunately, HBS backstops its students with the prestige of the degree, the wisdom of the professors, the experience of give-and-take classroom discussions, and the confidence that comes from finishing a difficult program successfully. All this helps generate a personal resiliency and the ability to adapt when situations are stressful. A good bit of luck also helps.

DEALING NARCOTICS
Soft-spoken Don Mottinger certainly accepted some of the toughest challenges in advancing his career. A graduate of the University of Idaho and a Navy officer, he moved to California in 1970 to work with an electronics company. Nothing particularly exciting about

that, but after three years, the company spun off a pharmaceutical business and asked Don to move to Los Angeles and be chief financial officer. His new office was in the Watts section of Los Angeles, which later became nationally known for its riots. Don was the only white person working with 40 local, black employees distributing narcotic pharmaceuticals. Their main drug product had a $6,000 market value but a $700,000 street value. Don handled this job for 2½ years through regular robberies and the killing of two company guards, all the while knowing that his life was largely dependent on a button under his desk linked directly to the police station.

His next job was in the credit department for Xerox, where his main responsibility was to chase and collect money from movie studios and dead-beat lawyers. He did this successfully for four years before joining Western Gear in Los Angeles, working as a manager in a division building transmissions for jet engines. After eight years, it was acquired. Next, he was asked to move to Cleveland in 1988 to become president of Lear Sigler Power Equipment Corp. Two weeks after his arrival in Cleveland, he had a surprise visit at his plant from more than a dozen government employees threatening to shut the operation down for poor quality work under government contracts. At the same time, he had to deal with five FBI investigators looking into fraud. A disgruntled employee with a grudge had turned whistle-blower. He survived this by proving the government was under-billed, not over-billed. Over the next four years, he built annual sales from $45 million to $120 million while reducing headcount from 1,200 to 700.

In 1992, he refused a company request to transfer back to California. Instead, he bought a small firm in Cleveland, Superior Screw, with 22 employees and $2 million in sales. In 2011, it had 90 employees and $12 million in revenue. The variety of these career challenges didn't overwhelm Don, who offered this advice: "Try to understand what you're good at, not what's in vogue, and make sure it fits you." His biggest dread now is retirement.

FIGHTING FOR SUCCESS

Jack Curry was another grad who pursued a difficult path. Jack considers himself perhaps the least likely admit to the HBS Class of 1970. He was a war baby born to a 17-year-old Irish/English father and a 16-year-old Ashkenazi Jewish mother. His parents grew apart during WW II and ultimately divorced and married others. He left home at the age of 16 and used his football prowess to attend three different colleges and earn a degree. Before being accepted at HBS, he was in the Army and had a brief stint at Standard Oil. He remains grateful to Tony Athos, the HBS professor who helped choose members of the class, for taking a chance on him. He arrived in Boston penniless.

In his first month at HBS, his name was in the newspaper after being mugged in Cambridge. He faced other fights after he graduated. First, he took a job with a Boston accounting firm to support a new wife and child, but lost it six months later after a merger forced layoffs. Next, he ran a small real estate firm that owned medical office buildings and some apartments. It went bankrupt. He joined a larger real estate development firm as a project manager, but it also went bankrupt. Each time, a burly Jack dusted himself off and got back into the game.

In 1974, he formed a company with a big construction firm. In 1983, they agreed to split the company into a development company and a management company. He got the management side, and as CEO, grew it to 330 employees handling 10,000 apartments in New England, New York, and Indiana. He also pursued development projects, but did so with a very conservative financial approach. He wouldn't guarantee loans or cross- collateralize holdings. He arranged non-recourse mortgages, and most important, he didn't take risks he couldn't afford. Jack said he worked on the premise that "if you take care of the property, it will take care of you."

Jack continued as a real estate operator with special attention paid to keeping his customers happy. He used the same approach with people, offering good benefits and paying out 20% of the profits to employees. "I have good people and I delegate well," he said. "People will work hard if you leave them alone." He forms small groups to solve problems and likes to move quickly. A financially successful and enjoyable life has been his reward.

OUTSTANDING IN HIS FIELD

For Bob Kerr, unfortunate timing caused a flop on his first farming venture but didn't prevent his ultimate success. "It takes a long time for something different to catch on," was Bob's observation. This was the hard lesson he learned as he closed the doors in 2008 after a nine-year effort to introduce organic beef to consumers. Bob knew he would face challenges, since his herd of 1,700 grass-fed beef cattle in southern Ontario, Canada, was no economic match for the 100,000-head grain feed lots in Texas, Nebraska, and Alberta. His natural beef, raised without hormones or antibiotics, was healthier for consumers but needed a 15–20% premium price to be profitable. It was easy to get the premium on choice steak cuts, but proved impossible for hamburger and lesser cuts of meat. The market just wasn't there, and he stopped supplying a Toronto store featuring grass-fed meat just a week before newspapers were filled with articles about mad cow disease in Great Britain.

Luckily for Bob, a second-generation farmer, other aspects of his farming business were more successful. He initially grew seed corn, sugar beets, and soy beans on 600 acres, but soon added organic asparagus. He also grew tomatoes for Heinz on a contract basis. He added more acres to his farm and moved to organic farming on about half his 1,500 acres. His neighbors thought this was foolish, but low prices and marginable profitability on conventionally grown produce just couldn't match the profits available from organic farming. Heinz asked for organic squash for its baby food line. Organic wheat was sent to Evergreen Juices for its wheat grass health drinks. He expanded his asparagus, added green beans, and produced organic corn for chicken farmers. Customers like Whole Foods welcomed his healthy produce into their stores.

Looking back on the unsuccessful effort to introduce natural grass-fed beef into the market, Bob offered a quote from Machiavelli: "There is nothing more difficult...., or more uncertain in its success, than to take the lead in the introduction of a new order of things, because the innovator has for enemies all those who have done well under the old conditions, and lukewarm defenders in those who may do well under the new."

AVOIDING DISGRACE

Sometimes success in a business career can take an abrupt downturn without warning. In the case of George McClelland, he might have wound up in financial disgrace had he not made a tough personal decision to do what he knew was right.

It was 1991 and George had 20 years of financial successes working with Data General and Fidelity Investments when he got a new job offer. Henry Burkhardt, George's former boss at Data General, had founded Kendell Square Research and wanted George to take the position of chief operating officer with the CFO reporting to him. At the time, Kendell was one of the best performing stocks on the New York Stock Exchange. It had tremendous technology and seemingly could make no mistakes. George signed on.

On his first day on the job, George saw the accounts receivable were lengthening and asked for the sales files since the company went public so he could take them home and review them. Most did not have the documents necessary to claim the sales as true revenue. At a meeting of senior executives, promises to provide those documents were made but they were never delivered. He then discovered supercomputers sitting on the shipping docks that were supposed to have been shipped and sold. George had confirmed that the books were being cooked.

George had to blow the whistle on the company and resigned within three weeks. The stock, which had jumped when he joined, was down 32% when he left. A federal investigation followed and the SEC charged Mr. Burkhardt with fraud for issuing materially false and misleading financial statements. He was forced to resign and paid $1.1 million in penalties and was barred from acting as an officer or director at any public company for ten years.

George had to answer many questions, but was not penalized because he had done what he was required to do even though the experience was most unpleasant. He lost a large personal investment in the stock, as did many shareholders when the company went bankrupt a year later. Kendell's corporate rise and fall later became an HBS case study.

Happier memories came from his first 15 years at Data General. Starting in 1972, in anticipation of leaving the Air Force, George sent five separate letters to the CEO asking to be interviewed for a job. When he finally got invited, he was told the company had no suitable position for him. Thinking fast, he suggested he could expand Data General's business worldwide. He got the chance. As international controller, he was instrumental in leading the computer company outside U.S. markets and into 62 different countries. Data General quickly grew, with revenues increasing at 63% annually for the first 10 years. Employees worldwide went from 400 to 20,000, and Data General became #211 on the Fortune 500 list of largest companies by sales.

Before he became treasurer in 1977, George was spending 50% of his time traveling internationally. "Titles meant nothing," he remembered of this entrepreneurial growth phase, when he wore many hats for his differing duties. "Senior management shared one tie, worn by whoever was going to a meeting that day." He was willing to take risks and see what he could accomplish, an opportunity that his classmates working with larger and more established organizations didn't usually have.

He has continued to take entrepreneurial risks since 1991, starting a securities lending firm that shifted the power in a $2 trillion industry away from custodians and to those who owned the stock inventory such as pension funds. He sold the company six years later for 20 times his investment. He also helped found a voice authentication company, a currency management firm, and later F-Squared Investments, an institutional investment management company where two world-class mathematicians helped him see superior returns with less risk. Nor have his talents been limited to business. He served on the board of the University of Massachusetts Medical School from 1985 to 1998, the last six years as its chairman. By serving a six-state New England market and growing to 15 associated campuses from only one in Worcester, Massachusetts, he increased revenue from $146 million to $760 million. The hospital was the first in the area to offer life-flight helicopters, and established three biotech parks to become a leading research facility. He's especially proud of giving doctors the authority to initiate programs that might decrease costs and improve patient outcomes.

GO WITH THE FLOW

Perhaps the most difficult career start was that of Mike Manis. Mike was determined to work in southern California after graduation, but not many companies there made the trip to Boston to recruit. Mike took the initiative and tracked down a decent size real estate developer in the San Diego area and convinced him over the phone to offer a job. In June, 1970, Mike packed up a new VW for the trip west, taking time to see the country as he went. When he arrived in San Diego, he went to his new employer's office and found a bankruptcy sign on the door.

For three months, he scrambled with odd jobs, then moved to Los Angeles, got his real estate license, and sold income properties to limited partnerships. He earned only $9,000 over an 18-month period. In 1975, he became VP of marketing for a golf course developer near Hilton Head, South Carolina. After four months, he came back to Los Angeles. He spent some time selling real estate and worked for a company organizing trips for golfers. In 1978, he wanted a steadier job, so he took a position teaching real estate principles, finance, and ethics at a local community college. He supplemented his teacher's salary with other jobs, and at one point was working four jobs at the same time.

In 1981, Mike published a book on real estate investing, but book sales collapsed when community colleges in California decided to no longer give credits for real estate courses. About this time, he got married and moved to Palm Springs. He taught general management and accounting at a community college near his new home for 20 years.

Mike is now retired and as he reflected on his career, he acknowledged he was happy but not a major financial success. This doesn't bother him. "There's no need to apologize for your career choices," he said. "Don't get locked into your first choice, since your circumstances will change. Go with the flow and be flexible."

WORKING UNTIL YOU CAN'T

Another classmate also scrambled through his business career, but had the additional challenge of being responsible for two families. As a former Marine who didn't graduate from HBS until he was 33 years old, George Katsarakas was not afraid to take on tough assignments. He started his business career as a management consultant. He also opened a Boston restaurant that failed when parking proved inadequate. Rockwell International hired him in 1973 to manage a textile machinery company selling a new type of cotton yarn equipment. The business suffered heavy losses when textile manufacturing moved overseas. George oversaw the liquidation of a one-million-square-foot plant and everything in it.

He took a new job in Texas as general manager for a sprinkler company, and then moved to New York in 1978 as plant manager for Otis Elevator, a unit of United Technologies, with responsibility for several thousand employees. He quickly discovered the Japanese were making competitive motors and selling them for less than his material costs at Otis. By taking on new business products, he kept the plant open for three years before it was closed. Pratt & Whitney then hired him as general manager for their jet engines and aircraft composites business, and he remained there for ten years.

A five-year stint followed as executive VP for manufacturing and engineering at Eagle Electric on Long Island. He then moved as chief operating officer to Network Technologies in the same town. This company produced surge suppressors to protect hard-line telephone systems. In 2001, cell phones started replacing fixed phones, and hard-line telephone companies suffered. The company went from employing thousands to a payroll of just 66.

Also in 2001, George, who had divorced and remarried a younger woman, became the father of twins at age 63. The costs of a second family, difficulty finding a new job, and illness in the extended family prompted a personal bankruptcy filing in 2010. George now works with a friend in Massachusetts as manager of four fitness gyms with 25,000 members. The position permits him to work out regularly, which he does at least three times a week.

At age 75, when interviewed, he said he planned to stay active "and work until I can't." His main regret is having two families needing him. "When children are involved, stay in a marriage," he advised others. Despite the challenges he's faced and faces, he said, "I'd trade nothing of what I have for all the money in the world."

Dodging Punches

England-born classmate Bill Hadman wandered the world during his career, dodging the business punches that were thrown his way. Initially, he looked for what he called a "proper job" in his motherland, first with a construction firm's painting contracting unit and then running its scaffolding business until the parent firm decided to close it. He moved to join Bowater Corporation as a business development executive and spent time from 1973 to 1981 in South Korea, Japan, and Kenya. Although he had married and officially was based in the United Kingdom, for three years he looked after African commodity plantations and trading operations, especially involving coffee.

For the next 15 years, he worked for International Paint, initially in Saudi Arabia where he supervised a mainly Indian workforce. While there, his company's factory burned down. The local police were convinced it was an act of religious sabotage and conducted a full-scale investigation. Bill finally persuaded the authorities that paint manufacturing was unstable at the high temperatures in the country (130 degrees Fahrenheit), and the fire was simply an unfortunate industrial accident. He was moved to India, where he set up and ran another paint factory. He said he dealt with the workforce by "treating people the way you would want to be treated."

One of his biggest scares came after he became a consultant in 1999 and took an assignment in Nigeria. His job resulted in making life uncomfortable for somebody who was subsequently evicted from a nearby building. That person had government contacts. Fortunately, Bill had friends. He was tipped off that he was about to be indicted for attempted assassination and fled the country just in time.

In 2009, Bill had a major setback when a motorcycle crash put him in a French hospital for almost five months. He came out with limited personal mobility. In reviewing his career, he said his regrets "are much greater for omission than commission." His advice for all is to "go for it."

HARD LUCK AND SUNSHINE

People might think that a career spent working in Hawaii would be ideal. Not necessarily so. "I had a careen, not a career," admitted Jay "Duke" Lembeck, a 1970 HBS grad living in Hawaii who returned for his 30th reunion in Boston courtesy of a classmate who paid for his plane ticket. Duke figured he held 43 jobs during his first 43 years after graduation, most related to real estate.

During the summer before graduation, Duke found a perfect job working in the Bahamas as an assistant to the president of Resorts International, a well-known resort development firm. He traveled throughout the Caribbean, much of which reminded him of the Hawaiian island of Oahu where he was raised. After graduation and a brief stint in New England, he returned to the Caribbean in 1972 as an assistant manager for a resort and casino developer. "I didn't know it was run by the Mafia," he said, "until I learned the manager was skimming profits, as required by his boss so the company would under report income."

Duke decided that Miami would be a good place to relocate. He worked as a mortgage banker and was doing well since one-third of all U.S. housing starts were recorded in Florida in early 1973. Unfortunately, Florida decided there was too much growth and shut-off any further water hook-ups for new homes. This froze the housing market. Duke returned to Oahu and got another job as a mortgage banker.

The new job lasted only a short time before Duke began covering the job alphabet: appraiser, broker, consultant, developer, environmental planner, feasibility analyst, etc. In 1982, he joined with a CPA to syndicate Montana properties to raise cattle. He quit in his first year and watched as his bosses went to jail for defrauding investors. It turned out there were no cattle. An agricultural partnership in Hawaii also went nowhere. In 1985, he tried being a commercial and industrial real estate broker. Things were going well since he was paid a salary and brought in the firm's biggest deal, but the company ran out of money and closed down.

In 1986, Duke returned to his high school job as a beach boy to make divorce payments to his ex-wife. He paddled tourists around Oahu for a fee. A few years later, he was working as an advisor to Hawaii's Board of Land and Natural Resources, the powerful government overseer of Hawaii's development projects. He made the mistake of opposing a building permit for a garish mansion with two-foot-thick concrete walls to be painted with glistening marble-chip paint and situated on a hillside above Oahu. The intended owner, a politically influential figure, was not pleased. Duke lost his job.

He made another mistake in 1994 when he crossed a union picket line. The union put him on the short list of six people, which itself was a subset of a black list of 600 people. "The unions in Hawaii are very powerful," Duke observed. He quickly became ineligible for getting any real estate or governmental job and learned if someone did hire him, that person would incur the wrath of the unions. "I was on a roller coaster, in part because I was prideful and disrespectful," he said.

In weighing the pluses and minuses of his career, Duke found some bright spots. He enjoyed substitute teaching in private schools, had roles in some commercials and a movie, was part of a winning outrigger racing team, visited all eight major Hawaiian Islands, and sailed and paddled frequently. "I had a lot of fun, but I missed the boat on my career," he said. When asked what he'd change, his only regret was that he didn't stay married. He said his three divorces were his fault. At age 70, he planned to leave Hawaii for California, where his 93-year-old father was fighting Alzheimer's disease and his stepmother said she could use some help.

Moving On

The 1964 Civil Rights law offered no protection against gender discrimination, a fact Kazie Metzger learned before attending HBS. When preparing to graduate from Duke University, she was interviewed for a job at RCA and was told, "We don't hire women for our training program." She decided to go to business school instead. Stanford University told her, "We don't actively recruit women." She applied to and was accepted by Harvard, which now has 42% women in its MBA classes.

Upon graduation, she was in debt and was looking for a safe career choice to allow her to repay her obligations. She had two offers from banks and took one of them. She regrets she didn't schedule more interviews to know what was available. She went into a training program for commercial lending but lost her job after nine months when the bank decided to reduce head count. She took another bank job in the back office, but left in late 1972 to join RCA.

She remained with RCA for seven years, working in global communications, especially trying to move cable television channels to foreign markets via satellites. She then joined Group W Cable in strategic planning, and remained there until 1986 when the business was sold. She and three others started a new company to distribute programming to satellite dishes, but four years later investors "squeezed out" the four founders.

Her background and her husband's 14 years of inventing offered an alternate job: litigating to protect his 100-plus patents, most related to smart set-top boxes and transmission methods that included signals sent to TVs, computers, smart phones, etc. "Creating a considerable revenue stream may be possible, but you have to be able to hang on and litigate for a long time," she said.

Looking back at the challenges she faced having both a career and a family, she admitted it wasn't easy: "I was on airplanes all the time, but at first my husband worked at home and a caretaker came in." Later, her husband worked with patent lawyers in Washington, D.C., for four years and commuted home on weekends, making scheduling more difficult. She estimated that 75% of the 29 women in the Class of 1970 got married and about half had children. "Staying involved with the children is worthwhile, but if you stay out of the workforce too long you lose your credibility," she said.

She counsels people to "think through what you'd like to do and what will make you happy, but don't feel bad if you don't have a career mapped out in advance." And "When you're not learning anything, it's time to move on," she added.

CURING HIMSELF

Working in the medical innovation area for 25 years was helpful but not nearly enough for Bruce Lottman when he encountered his own health challenge in the mid-'90s. Bruce knew he had a problem as his energy levels dropped, but nobody was able to identify the cause. "I did a lot of rule in/rule out personal trials, and got my blood chemistry done to relate to my genomic make-up. This knowledge saved my life," he said, as he tailored a drug program to his genetic profile. Bruce believes an individual needs to take control of his own life. "I had to put aside business and learn enough medicine to cure myself."

Earlier in his life, Bruce spent ten years after HBS working with Beckman Instruments, Baxter, and the medical part of Litton Industries. With big company experience in his background, he was asked to run a company trying to improve on the detection of breast cancer. After five years the effort failed, but Bruce was not discouraged. "You learn more lessons in a failure," he said. "You should embrace it." He then joined a genetics company, but after 18 months the controlling venture capitalist sold it. After this, he worked in the areas of venture capital and consulting before his own medical problem hit. Bruce was lucky compared to another classmate he knew well. The other individual declined an interview, but had started and sold two successful medical companies before he was playing in a racquetball tournament and his body went numb. He had to move into a full-time nursing facility and has been battling to regain movement in his arms and legs. Nothing is as cruel or career-ending as an extreme and undiagnosed medical problem.

Reflecting on his life, Bruce believes that experience equals wisdom, but its value is often underestimated. He noted that venture capitalists look for people with big company successes, but they should be looking for entrepreneurial managers instead. He advised business people not to "rush for the top of the corporate ladder." Instead, he urged people to "figure out what you have a passion for and pursue that, not money." Even then, timing is critical to a person's success. "You can be right and end up failing, but you need to learn from the experience."

STARTING A BANK

For 34 years, Thos Muller used his HBS training to handle various financial positions with distinction. In year 35, however, he was backed into a corner as chairman of the board of Net Bank, a $5 billion internet bank that was founded in 1996 and went public in 1997. This bank started in Atlanta and did some auto and equipment lending, but the bulk of its loan portfolio was in residential real estate. It was the first internet-only bank according to Thos. It grew rapidly, and added to its portfolio by acquiring a mortgage banking operation in South Carolina. When the housing crisis hit in 2006, the bank realized its costs were too high for its business model. "We should have focused earlier on how to leverage up with the cost structure we had," Thos said. Although not a bank employee, as chairman he faced both shareholder and FDIC lawsuits, and the bank was turned over to the FDIC for liquidation in 2007. "I'd be cautious about being on a board with any political or regulatory component," Thos warned.

Thos reflects on how quickly these problems arose. In quieter times, he wrote a thesis on starting a banking business, but put it aside to join Coca Cola in 1970. He stayed for 14 years, serving in the planning office, worked in marketing, and eventually becoming CFO for the wine business and later the domestic soft drink business. After leaving Coke in 1984, he worked as a CFO for several startups, including a healthcare software firm that grew from $60 million to $210 million before it was sold. He also worked on startups in the beverage business, telecommunications, and the medical device area. If he had a chance now to change his career, he said he would have left his banking thesis to gather dust.

FAILURE FIRST, THEN SUCCESS

Mike Makar had an idealistic approach to business that fit in well with the '60s. After college, he worked for the Job Corps for three years before moving on to HBS. After finishing his MBA, he joined Rouse & Co., then working on a "New Town" project in Columbia, Maryland (15 miles south of Baltimore). The idea was to take a large piece of land and put in extensive parks, recreation, and a shopping center to make an ideal setting for housing. Thus, a new and ideal town would be created from scratch. The property could eventually hold 150,000 people, but initially attracted only 15,000. With the infrastructure spending all put in up-front, economic pressures quickly appeared. Mike's boss chose to move ahead, using fraudulent financial projections to attract loans. Mike recalled that "things being done for the social good switched to things being done only if financially viable." Mike transferred to another office to work on regional shopping centers for Rouse. Three years after he left, lenders had to write off more than $100 million in loans on the "New Town" project.

After 4½ years with Rouse, Mike joined Connecticut General to invest in real estate equity and loans on its behalf. In 1978, he moved back to the Seattle area where he grew up and started a commercial mortgage banking business employing 20 people. He later sold it to Ranier Bank. When Security Pacific bought Ranier Bank, he bought his original business back and made it quite profitable, selling it later to C.B. Ellis and joining that firm as executive VP. He retired in 2012.

"I wasn't anxious to build a national company, but I did finance a lot of projects in downtown Seattle," Mike remembered. "I preferred to be part of a community that I really knew well. I wanted a sense of community and to do something I liked."

FINDING WHAT WORKS

Like a lot of HBS grads, Canadian Lindsay Eberts had a tough business start and a bumpy career path but eventually finished a winner. He did this, he said, by "working long enough and hard enough" and trying different things until he found something that worked.

Lindsay left HBS without a job because few Canadian companies recruited there and he wanted to return to Canada. He went to Toronto and joined a startup venture capital fund that couldn't raise enough capital and shut down. He then became president of a manufacturer of hockey sticks, learning on the job that the firm was targeting a high-end market with low-quality products. He hadn't done enough due diligence and the company was in serious trouble when he joined. His job was to close the main plant four months after arriving. The workers were so upset that he said he had to "run for my life."

He moved into banking with Guaranty Trust of Canada as assistant to the vice chairman, later becoming VP of marketing and planning and then moving to Vancouver as a lending officer. After six years, he became a land developer in the United States, working on strip malls and single-family homes. He was working in Fort Worth, Texas, in 1987 when the collapse of oil prices and many

Texas banks wiped out his personal equity. "You can't deal in the cyclical real estate business with 100% leverage without getting wiped out when the market turns," he said. "You can't borrow your way out of debt."

He wasn't ready to give up, so in 1992 he moved to Seattle and joined Seattle Aero as a 50% partner with the firm's founder owning the other half. The firm assembled retrofit kits for B-737s and B-757s, sourcing U.S. parts to support the Japanese aerospace industry. Business really boomed when the firm started selling winglets to attach to planes. These winglets improved fuel efficiency by 3½–5%. He started other businesses, including wheelchair lifts for buses and an import firm to bring gift items made in China into the United States. He sourced his own knock-offs and designs from 40–50 Chinese factories and built a $5 million sales company with only five employees. The employees received 25% of the gross profits as an incentive.

Looking back on his career, he said, "There were enormous highs and lows. You get lucky if you have persistence and the ability to stay in the ring. You need to build a team of supporters around you, not necessarily the big guys, because the little guys when given a chance will jump through hoops for you."

SUPPORTING THE LAW

For the first eight years of his career, Joe Burke served as the general manager of the WS Tyler division of Combustion Engineering. This Cleveland-based unit had multiple plants and sold large, engineered pieces of equipment worldwide, mostly to mining companies. Joe was doing well and decided he'd try to buy the division from the parent. When senior management reviewed the results, they decided it was too good to sell, and Joe moved on to work with four other companies over the next 12 years. The last of these was a trucking firm in Michigan owned by what he called two "Wall Street types" who brought him in as president. The firm needed to raise cash and Joe was told to sign a falsified cash flow statement to get a loan. He refused and was fired that day.

With a bad taste in his mouth from that experience, he became administrative manager for a New York City/New Jersey law firm with 70 lawyers. He did this for ten years before retiring. Looking back, Joe advised others not to be impetuous. "Take your time making decisions. Sometimes the people who you think stand in your way really don't."

MAINTAINING PEACE OF MIND

Being flexible is a necessary character trait for classmates who found their career paths anything but smooth. One of these was Terry Chapin, whose youthful appearance might have held him back if it weren't for his MBA. "HBS was my gold card," he remembered. He started with Arthur Young, the large accounting firm that was then looking to hire non-accounting majors to add more diversity to their offices. He spent time taking special accounting courses before joining the Los Angeles office on the audit side. After 1½ years with the firm, he decided the job wasn't for him.

He moved to be the financial person for a real estate developer building apartments and condos in Santa Monica, but the firm was in the trouble and its parent company dissolved it. He spent seven years with a data management software company, then left to become VP of finance for a specialty restaurant company with 70 locations around the country. After two years, he became law firm administrator for an LA office with 100 lawyers for another two years. Next, was VP of finance for the fast-food operation Orange Julius before it was sold after three years to Dairy Queen, which then installed its own people. Another law firm administrator job lasted only a year because the 80-lawyer firm dissolved itself after it lost Johnny Carson as a client. He joined a Beverly Hills entertainment law firm as administrator, got his real estate license, and moved to yet another job as a law firm administrator. In 1994, he finally found stability as CFO for a family foundation running a variety of investments.

Terry said his career "got to be a joke because the firms kept folding or otherwise going out of business." Despite the many bumps in the road, he kept his focus on being emotionally content. "I sacrificed money for a good family situation, and maintained my peace of mind."

Out of Focus

Bernie Skown had a West Point education and six years in the Army behind him when he entered HBS. After earning his MBA, he spent two years with General Cable as a market analyst before joining Time, Inc. with production responsibilities to get books and magazines out on time. His boss lost out in a promotion battle, and Bernie's days at Time were numbered. He moved to Grolier as director of corporate planning in 1975. The firm encountered financial difficulties and the CEO was fired. The new CEO didn't need Bernie. The next eight years were more promising as Bernie joined an English paint-making subsidiary in Detroit and helped sales grow from $30 million to $100 million. He was working as assistant to the company's CEO and did a bunch of things, allowing him to learn a lot about how smaller companies operate.

In 1986, he bought a small New Jersey company doing $5 million in sales. The seller kept working for the company, and later was discovered taking kickbacks from suppliers. Bernie considers himself lucky in getting his money back. The next ten years he worked in consulting, including a job in former Soviet Union countries converting defense buildings to other uses. In 2000, he joined the faculty of Stevens Institute of Technology, a New Jersey engineering school. He got a "best teacher" award for starting a business and technology program at the school. He retired in 2011. Looking back at his career, Bernie said, "I never really was focused on what I wanted to do." He advised others that when in doubt on which company to join, go with the more established company. He pointed out, "It's easier to move from a large company to a small one rather than the other way."

TIRED OF TRAVELING

Before he came to HBS, Matt Maury had worked three years in wood product sales for Weyerhauser, spending time in Tacoma, Atlanta, and New Orleans. Upon graduation, he went back to Weyerhauser's headquarters in Tacoma, but after 1½ years was moved to Charlotte for two years and then back to Tacoma to work in corporate planning. In 1980, at the age of 40 and with a family that included four children, he was tired of traveling extensively and of office politics. When he was offered a chance to head up Japanese sales, he refused and started looking for something else to do.

What he found was "The Homeowners' Club," a membership organization that suggested reliable contractors for home repairs. He and his wife bought the club and charged members in the King County area of Tacoma an annual $54 fee plus a percentage of the work billed. He guaranteed satisfaction, and made sure the homeowner was happy before the contractor was paid. He said the much larger contractor referral service, Angie's List, doesn't guarantee the work done and contractors can move up the list by buying advertising. Even though the company stayed only in the local area, seven employees were added. Matt's career move from major company employee to small firm entrepreneur was personally very satisfying. He explained, "I come to work every day because I like to. When I was with Weyerhauser, I became so focused on my career that I overlooked my family and friends. I loved what I was doing but I was missing my wife and my kids growing up."

HBS BY CANDLELIGHT

Tom Feeley spent six years in the Army and had reached the rank of captain in the Airborne Ranger group before a friend talked him into applying to HBS. At the time, Tom was serving as an adviser to the South Vietnamese. Without a typewriter, he hand-wrote his application by candlelight. He was accepted.

Just before graduating from HBS, a friend of Tom's couldn't make a campus interview with jeans maker Levi Strauss, so Tom went to the interview and was hired to join the marketing staff in San Francisco. As the company grew from $250 million to $2.5 billion in annual sales and went public, Tom was moved back to New England and worked as sales manager for that territory from 1973 to1980. He then left the company to consult for the garment business, but when that didn't work out, he moved into real estate as a commercial tenant representative, earning a fee as the building owner's contact with tenants. Tom advised others to "follow your own instincts and be a change-oriented person." He also warned, "Don't try to compare yourself to other people."

OVERCOMING DEMONS

Another classmate who performed military service before entering HBS was Sandy Creighton, who spent five years in Vietnam on an underwater demolition team as a Navy Seal before that term was used. After he finished, he spent eight months traveling around the world before entering HBS. What he didn't know, and only learned 15 years later after psychological testing, was that he had suffered post-traumatic stress during the war. He said, "I had a lack of self-esteem, and came back guilty that I was still alive."

Sandy went to work in Boston with Cabot, Cabot & Forbes developing real estate. He focused on the safety of high-rise buildings, noting that the Hancock Tower is like a city with 30,000 people working there. He developed safety drills and trained people to prepare for any emergency. In 1978, he moved to Portland, Oregon, to run a real estate development firm, and three years later started his own company redeveloping historic buildings on the West Coast. He then was project manager for the Silicon Valley Financial Center, working for the Campeau Corporation. In 1987, Prudential hired him in Boston to downsize its $9 billion office and industrial real estate portfolio. This risk reduction effort led to selling a lot of buildings, especially to Japanese joint ventures, according to Sandy.

For the next 16 years, he worked on various real estate projects, many involving the telecom industry, with multiple employers. In 2008, pushing 70 years of age, he became licensed to sell life insurance for New York Life and became a member of the million-dollar roundtable. Sandy said he "looks back with gratitude for coming out the other side" and overcoming the demons that troubled him after the war. "I have a spiritual self-awareness now. I finally found peace with myself."

SELL OUTS

Canadian Dave Alsop climbed to the top of two different companies, only to watch his hard work be destroyed by outside influences. Dave initially joined McKinsey & Co. as a consultant in Toronto. After spending three years with them, his wife noted that "your new daughter doesn't recognize you." He quit consulting and was recruited to North Vancouver to join Cornat Industries, a conglomerate. He worked for the ship-building unit Burrard Yarrows Corporation for 17 years, the last three as CEO overseeing two shipyards and 3,000 employees. When the parent company got into financial difficulty, money was drained from Dave's unit until it was sold. Dave left to become CEO of a troubled truck manufacturing company that built trucks and also acquired truck parts at a discount and sold them at retail prices. In two years, he cut costs and was beginning to make money when the owner, a British multinational trading company located in Singapore, sold it out from under him.

Dave's next step was to look to buy a company, but he found nothing worthwhile after spending two years and looking at over 100 companies. In 1994, he became president of Vancouver Wharves, a bulk shipping terminal. He took it from breakeven to profitable for its owner B.C. Rail, which then asked him to serve as interim CEO for WesTel, a telecommunications company also owned by the railroad. He was CEO for three years when a New York global communications company bought it, changed its name to RSL Communications, Canada, and asked Dave to stay as CEO. Dave expanded the microwave and wireless services as well as land lines, and eventually its reach covered 60% of the Canadian population. RSL's parent, however, ran into financial problems and went into receivership. Dave left and worked with two small companies before retiring in 2008.

Looking back, Dave was glad to get the turnaround experience and move from industry to industry without the need to physically move his family. He now serves as president of a community corporation, owns a small company, and plays golf with scores in the '80s. His biggest success, however, he said was his family—wife, daughter, and granddaughter.

A WRITING CAREER

Headed for Hollywood was the career intent of Tom Caplan, who spent the summer between his business school years working for an executive VP at MGM Studio. His plans changed suddenly when Kirk Kerkorian bought MGM and fired top management. Tom stayed in Boston to write a novel and become writer-in-residence at the Harvard College dormitory Elliott House. After two years, he moved back to his hometown of Baltimore to work, on and off, for 23 years in the family jewelry business.

He described his work as "doing everything" in the whole-sale/retail jewelry business. This included selling a novel ("Line of Chance") published in 1979 about a fictitious 19th century jewelry swindle.

He continued to work and write, and spent a great amount of time in London, both dealing in jewelry and researching future novels, including "Parallelogram." In 1991–1992, he worked as a speech writer for his Georgetown roommate Bill Clinton and traveled with him on the campaign trail. He helped Clinton on three speeches that set forth his positions on personal responsibility, economic policy, and foreign affairs. After the campaign, he returned to Baltimore where, as an only child, he cared for a dying mother and his father who had Parkinson's disease. He also published his third novel, "Grace and Favor." While continuing with speech writing for President Clinton after Clinton left office, he published his fourth novel, "The Spy Who Jumped from the Screen."

Tom says he was extremely lucky to get to HBS. He had been in ROTC and expected to be sent to Vietnam, but was hit on the head at boot camp and washed out of the service. "Little things can have a major effect on your life," he observed. His father has died, and Tom has set his sights on writing a book a year.

JOINING THE FAMILY BUSINESS

Chuck Fienning was unsure what path to take after graduation, so he decided to stay for a year at HBS as a research assistant. He moved on in 1971 to join a Danish steamship company in New York for what he thought was a job to set up a real estate investment trust. Instead, he was moved to a manufacturing subsidiary and spent most of his time on the road. This was not what he was promised, so he left in 1973 to start a mobile home sales company with a partner in North Carolina. High interest rates and a weak economy worked against success for the business. At Chuck's fifth HBS reunion, he discovered he was in the bottom decile of the class in both income and wealth according to an informal class poll.

By 1977, he left his partner in charge of the business and moved to Illinois to join his father's corrugated box business. He lived at home and was $50,000 in debt. When he attended his 15th high school reunion, he met the girl he would soon marry. The newly-weds were transferred to South Carolina, where Chuck became a salesman for Sumter Packaging Company, part of the family business. When annual sales fell from $3 million to $2 million, he was made general manager of the firm with instructions to "save it or sell it." Chuck did the former by focusing on increasing cash flow. His efforts from 1984 to 1987 won him a local award in the business turn-around category. He credits his success to customer service. "You need to make the client not want to go somewhere else," he said.

Chuck served as CEO of Sumter Packaging for 25 years, grow-ing annual sales to $25 million. His son is now in charge of the company. Chuck continues to spend a fair amount of time as Sec-tion C correspondent for the HBS Class of 1970. He provides news monthly about 70 or so of his remaining section mates to boost friendships and collaboration. Section C has been the most cohe-sive group from the Class of 1970, "helping one another with advice and even financially," according to Chuck. There have been several mini-reunions for the section, including two at a classmate-owned vineyard in Napa, California. He said nobody in the Class of 1970 is happier than he is. "Success in life is about developing relation-ships, and we did that in Section C," he reported proudly.

A WOMAN'S WORLD

Colleen Burke came to HBS out of Vassar College as one of 29 women entering among the approximately 750 members of the Class of 1970. It was a lonely time for her, she said, especially since there was no opportunity to live on campus like the men. Instead, the women could get their own apartments or stay at Radcliffe's graduate school dorms across the Charles River. When the weather changed, the long walk became freezing and possibly dangerous late at night when returning from late campus study sessions, Colleen took action. She simply moved without authorization into the one room at HBS set aside as a women's retreat during the day.

This direct action prompted a meeting with Dean George Baker, who listened carefully to her concerns. He was persuaded to let Colleen and three other women, chosen by lottery, officially move onto the campus on January 1, 1969. To integrate the women into campus living, he asked the consulting firm Booz Allen to conduct a $250,000 study of what women needed in the dorms. For $250, Colleen did her own study and provided it to the school. Thus, she became an early pioneer for the 42% of women in classes now at HBS. She was also asked to offer advice on how the school should go about recruiting women into its doctorate program for business education, thus beginning a pipeline for future women professors at HBS.

Colleen spent her time during the '70s doing consulting and starting two small companies. The first was Saratoga Vichy Mineral Water Company, which was sold in 1978 to Anheuser-Busch. The second was the Children's Design Center, which reached $1 million in revenues in its first year. She also worked for a time as executive assistant to the chairman and CEO of Great Western United in Denver, a fast-growing Fortune 500 company. She left when she married her boss, a marriage that gave her a son but ended in divorce followed by ten years of litigation over the child's custody and the ownership of the two businesses she had founded.

After the litigation, Colleen became executive in residence for the Department of Management and Business at Skidmore College in upstate New York. She taught classes with the case study method used by HBS. She was honored by being asked to be Skidmore's graduation speaker in 1990, speaking on life in the business world. She continues to be active, both as a teacher and a consultant.

10

WHEN TIMES
ARE TOUGH

Nobody can avoid a scar or two as they move through 40-plus years of a business career. In the previous chapter on "Handling Adversity," you read about some typical problems: bad timing, dangerous job positions, corporate reorganizations, poor health, unfavorable family situations, excessive debt for a cyclical business, and changing bosses. These problems are common, and getting past them requires the right attitude and an ability to make the best of whatever situation you're in. It also helps to have flexibility, something that seems to be gained by most HBS graduates. The prestige of the MBA degree provides a chance to move forward out of the toughest of job situations into something else. Best of all, an alumna/alumnus remains in good standing even if a large contribution is not made to the school's annual fund drive.

Many of the people mentioned didn't let bad situations destroy them. Instead, they made the best of what they had, worked hard, did the right thing, and moved on to something better. They figured out what was required to improve their own situation. Sometimes it involved recognizing new trends to seize upon. Other times it was to select good people, delegate by giving authority with responsibility, and staying out of the way. Keeping one's personal life uncomplicated and avoiding bad partners and politics are also good paths to success. If you find yourself stagnant and not going anywhere, you need to take control of your own destiny and leave for something else.

One sign that it's time to move on is when you're not learning anything and you can't see changing that situation anytime soon. Sometimes office politics or simply too much traveling can prompt a departure. Don't worry about maintaining your status by keeping a job you don't like. Follow your own instincts and find something you can enjoy and work hard at without regret. Success can be achieved in many different ways, but only if you pursue it with enthusiasm.

11

WINNING ON
WALL STREET

THERE WAS NO BETTER CAREER path to financial success in the
'70s, '80s, and '90s than moving to New York City and finding a job on Wall Street. The financial markets were not
new, but after 1970, managing assets for others exploded in both
number of accounts and total dollars. There were also highly profitable innovations on Wall Street: junk bonds, option strategies, derivatives, mega-mergers, leveraged buyouts, money market funds,
international securities trading, mortgage-backed securities, venture
capital investing, etc. Those HBS classmates who jumped early into
this financial whirlpool and stayed with it were swept to prosperity undreamed of as students. At least three classmates became billionaires, and many others who spent at least 15 years working the
financial markets gained enough wealth so they didn't worry about
their next paychecks.

Already mentioned was Tony Berg, the Australian who worked
in New York for a brief period before returning to his homeland and

helping develop the international investment firm known as Macquarie. During the summer months between our first and second years, Tony had the idea to arrange regular lunches where top Wall Street execs spoke to a small group of HBS summer trainees. One of the latter was Tony's section mate, Mike Quinn.

RIDING THE BOOM

Mike was the first person in his family to finish college. When he was accepted by HBS, he didn't know the investment business even existed. Despite this unlikely background, he reached out to Professor Colyer Crum, the legendary teacher of investment management, when he needed a summer job. He got a position at Argus Research and attended each of the ten lunches the summer HBS trainees arranged. Included among the execs invited were the heads of Goldman Sachs, Salomon Brothers, William D. Witter, Smith Barney, Loeb Rhoades, and Dreyfus. All were eager to talk about business, their firms, and employment prospects. Dining was elegant at private dining clubs and classy restaurants, and the firms picked up the tab.

Mike's particular contribution to the lunches was inviting Howard Stein, then chairman of the Dreyfus Corporation, best known for its many mutual funds available to investors. Mike introduced him to the group at the exclusive 21 Club, selected by the speaker. None of the students had been in the restaurant before. The menu was very pricey, so they all followed Mr. Stein's lead and all ordered 21 Burgers, which cost $10 at the time (equivalent to about $60 today).

In the fall of 1969, as the second year at HBS was beginning, Mike responded to a request to schedule an HBS recruiting dinner hosted by Dreyfus where Howard Stein again spoke. This time, Mike reserved a private room at Locke-Ober's, unaware that blacks and women had traditionally been excluded from the restaurant. Both groups were included without incident. Afterwards, Howard Stein was in a hurry to catch a plane, so Mike drove him to the airport. He was later hired by Dreyfus, where he worked from 1970 to 1976. These were bad years for the stock markets, but good years for money market funds and fixed income and convertible stock funds, all of which Mike worked on. When he left, he was president of two mutual funds and the firm's senior investment person in the fixed income area.

From 1976 to 1983, he traded bonds for Donaldson, Lufkin & Jenrette, another prominent Wall Street firm. Mike borrows a line and describes it as "the most fun you can have with your clothes on." He also earned his CFA (Chartered Financial Analyst) certification. Soon, he became senior sales manager, making over $1 million a year.

That salary didn't stop Merrill Lynch from hiring Mike away to be sales manager on the fixed income side in New York with 100 salesmen reporting to him. In two years, he became national sales manager, then international sales manager with people from Japan and Europe also reporting to him. He helped start the currency and interest swap businesses, and led Merrill from a 6th-place spot in debt underwriting to the #1 spot from 1986 into the mid-'90s. Along the way, he saw how dangerous derivative products could be when, in 1987, Merrill Lynch lost $500 million in the mortgage-backed security business because it was improperly hedged. Mike was put in charge and turned the unit profitable again in 12 months.

The '90s were booming times for the stock business, with daily trading volume growing from 160 million shares in 1990 to 1.6 billion shares in 1996. Merrill's stock price grew 20 times. Mike became co-head of the global equity business. He then took on responsibility for the institutional money management business. In that position in 1996, he pushed his firm to buy Wells Fargo Advisors, known for its index funds, for $450 million. A senior executive committee turned down the deal. It was sold instead to Barclay's, which later sold it for $16 billion. In 1999, at the age of 52, Mike had enough and decided to retire and spend time investing his own money.

In looking back at his career, Mike admits that he was inordinately fortunate with both his choices and timing. He calls it a golden period, and bemoans the fact that since the year 2000 "even Republicans can't be trusted with our money." For people in the investment business, he said, "Integrity is a person's most valuable and saleable asset. You can profit by being a person of integrity." He was accidentally tested in the mid-'70s when a messenger came into Dreyfus and mistakenly left him with a bag containing $150 million in U.S. Government bearer bonds, owned by whoever held them. He had a private laugh and immediately returned the bag to the proper office. "When I survey the wreckage of careers of many folks I knew, it strikes me that being greedy and in a hurry for wealth, success, and power, is often a formula for failure," he commented.

He encouraged young employees to find a mentor, and senior people to be a mentor. In managing people, he urged: "Be demanding by setting high expectations, even if people think you're unfair. People are capable of doing so many things, but they have to be challenged to do them."

STARTING AS A STATISTICIAN

Mike had a section mate at HBS, Joe Fogg, who was much more familiar with Wall Street than Mike was. Joe's father was in the financial printing business, so new stock offerings and prospectuses (explaining the terms of financing for investors) were familiar to Joe at an early age. While in high school, he thought he'd be a lawyer, but after college and despite acceptance at several law schools, he decided he liked business better. He chose HBS and after two years and a summer job on Wall Street, he graduated as a Baker Scholar (top 5% of the class) and joined the corporate finance department of Morgan Stanley. At the time, Morgan Stanley wasn't the power it is today. It had a total of just 200 employees, $7 million in capital, an office in New York City, and a small office in Paris. Those starting in the corporate finance department were called "statisticians" and earned between $8,000 and $15,000 annually.

Within two years, the firm decided to grow and change. It bought a seat on the stock exchange floor and underwent a massive expansion, including starting a mergers and acquisitions department. Joe joined the new department and participated in the hostile takeover boom of 1978. In 1979, he became the youngest of the firm's managing directors. He was then made head of corporate finance and traveled over a million miles to open offices worldwide. During the '80s, he also led some of the largest acquisition deals ever done, including the $11 billion buyout of Gulf Oil, which at the time was a record. He saw Morgan Stanley itself go public in the mid-'80s and was made head of worldwide investment banking.

As sales and trading became much bigger contributors to profits than investment banking, Joe realized he was unlikely to be chosen to lead the firm. In 1993, despite having 1,200 people under his direction, he decided to retire while remaining active as an advisory director for five more years. His financial experiences at Morgan Stanley made it easy for him to transition into private equity and early-stage venture investments, often done with outside funding sources.

Today, Joe spends his time on his investments and fundraising for various Republican candidates in New York and Florida. In reflecting on his career, he is glad he joined the right firm, one founded on the principles of meritocracy and high ethical standards. He also said he was lucky to move into the mergers and acquisitions area as it began to boom.

BILLIONAIRE BUYOUTS

One of the Class of 1970 billionaires had an early false start before heading for Wall Street and using what he learned to return to his native Canada and become a major force in corporate buyouts.

Gerry Schwartz turned down several Wall Street offers and initially took a job in Miami with a land development company. He was attracted by the large number of stock options he was awarded, which he thought could make him $5 million to $10 million in about five years. Only months into his new job, he realized he hated it and was unlikely to become rich with the options. Fortunately for Gerry, the president of a major Wall Street firm left to open his own smaller company and invited Gerry to join him in September, 1970.

Gerry headed north and began working in corporate finance alongside future buyout king Teddy Forstmann. He continued for 1½ years before deciding the firm was too small. He moved on to Bear Stearns, where he remained until 1977. During this time, his office was next to that of Henry Kravis, who later left Bear Stearns to form the soon-to-be-famous KKR investment firm. After six years, Gerry also left Bear Stearns to start his own company. He returned to his hometown of Winnipeg, Manitoba, Canada to co-found Can-West, a firm that successfully made acquisitions to become a TV, radio, and newspaper company. With 50% ownership, Gerry worked for the company for seven years before selling his shares in 1984.

He used the proceeds to put $50 million into Onex, a Toronto-based partnership he and other investors formed to buy companies in private equity deals. He took the firm public in April, 1987, to raise $250 million so he could pursue larger deals. Gerry retained voting control of the company by holding super voting stock. The market crash of October, 1987, dropped Onex's shares from the $20 offering price to below $8. Over the next 29 years, the firm completed 75 acquisitions and the stock went (adjusted for four splits) to the equivalent value of over $220 per share.

Onex made acquisitions primarily with its own money from 1984 to 2003, but the large size of some deals prompted the need for outside money. Public pension funds were brought in as limited partners in four created funds, each of which had Onex accounting for 25–50% of the investment dollars. Onex now has 80 professionals on staff and a market cap exceeding $6 billion. Gerry serves as chairman and CEO and credits the low professional turnover to the firm's entrepreneurial style, collegial spirit, and the personal financial stake taken by management. Each member of the team is required to reinvest 25% of his pre-tax gains into Onex stock and hold those shares until retirement. In this way, he aligns the interests of his professionals with his shareholders.

While Gerry admits to making a lot of financial mistakes, the one he remembers best occurred when he was 20 years old. At the time, the Canadian Mint was making 300,000 special mint coin sets annually for collectors. These sets could be bought for $3 and, Gerry realized, later sold for as much as $40. He started buying massively and continued for five years, making more money than he dreamed possible. He soon learned the fickleness of government actions, however, when the Mint instituted a new policy of making as many mint sets as people wanted. Gerry watched his fortune shrink rapidly as the mint sets dropped to the face value of the coins, or $1.91 per set.

Gerry continues full-time work with Onex, traveling frequently and watching with admiration as Heather, his wife of 35 years, builds Indigo Books, the Canadian company she founded 15 years ago, to nearly $1 billion in revenue. She observed that 35% of all books are bought as gifts, so Indigo has created gift departments in its 100 large stores and 125 mall stores.

When asked to comment on how the United States eventually stops printing money and deals with its massive debt, he noted that a "democracy will always have inflation." He said from the 1850s to the early 1970s, the U.S. dollar did not meaningfully change in value. In 1974, however, when Nixon had Congress drop the gold standard, valuation of the currency dropped sharply and continues to decline today. He used a simple description to summarize and warn about what is happening: Inflation is the silent thief in the night.

PICTURE PERFECT

Hollywood and Wall Street couldn't be further from one another both in style and geography, but somehow Allen Adler combined the two to make a success out of his business career. Allen's first move after leaving HBS was to become the first security analyst on the "buy side" for S&P Intercapital, a New York-based investment firm oriented towards managing pension fund assets. While there, he was fortunate to be introduced to Alan Hirschfield, an investor with a particular expertise in the media business. Allen and Alan were asked to look at the then-troubled company Columbia Picture Industries, Inc. Their analytical write-up and financial plans for Columbia so impressed both the company's management and the firm's worrying bankers that both men were asked to run Columbia. A turn-around was accomplished by selling assets (TV, radio, and music publishing) and adding cable TV and the record business.

Allen remained at Columbia Pictures for five years as SVP of corporate development. His most daring move was buying a pinball company for $50 million when Columbia's stock had a market value of only $20 million. The pinball acquisition was a huge success. Allen left New York for Los Angeles to enter the movie production business with funding from 20th Century Fox. Soon after his move, Coca-Cola offered to buy Columbia in a cash or Coca-Cola stock deal. Allen wisely chose the latter, and watched as his new holdings surged in value during the '80s and '90s.

In 1983, Alan Hirschfield became CEO of 20th Century Fox and wanted Allen as its president. Before the deal could be finalized, billionaire Rupert Murdoch bought half of 20th Century Fox and fired Hirschfield. Subsequently, two other movie companies talked to Allen about leadership roles, but changes in management at these Hollywood firms hindered decision-making. Allen, who had successfully leveraged his stock investing beginning in mid-1983, had enough. He moved back to New York City in 1985 and married Frances Beatty.

They started a family, and he devoted his business time to investing in both public and private markets. He also became involved in working with non-government organizations, and now devotes 40% of his time to helping nonprofits. He observed that during his working life only three or four decisions made his career a financial success. He advised patience in building a career, and noted, "We all have periods when nothing good is happening. Being ready and flexible are key when coming out of the bad times."

A BUSINESS CARD COLLECTION

It took Bob Nau five years after graduation to make it to Wall Street, but he entered the investment business right after graduation by joining A.G. Becker in Chicago. After working in the area of mergers and acquisitions and raising capital for companies, he was moved to New York. In 1978, Warburg and Paribas bought his group from A.G. Becker to assist its European clients in working with U.S. companies. Bob chose instead to join Blyth, Eastman, Dillon, doing pretty much what he had been doing.

Three years later, Bob followed his boss to Salomon Brothers, where he headed the global bank capital markets group. A trading scandal rocked Salomon and prompted Warren Buffet to come in to oversee his investment in the firm. When Buffet proved less than generous in setting pay levels, Bob was one of three top investment bankers in 1995 who left Salomon for UBS, a Swiss-based investment bank. UBS's 35-person banking group was then acquired by American firm Donaldson, Lufkin & Jenrette, which in turn was soon sold to Credit Suisse.

Bob retired in 2001, and even though he himself was relatively consistent throughout his career in the type of work he was doing, in 30 years he worked for four firms and had ten different business cards to reflect the firms' name changes. "I was lucky in picking an industry that had a rising tide," he reflected, "and my boat rose with it." He acknowledged that he may have done better financially if he had gotten to New York earlier and joined Goldman Sachs or J.P. Morgan. Yet he has no regrets about his business path or his retirement. "Wall Street firms are becoming more like commercial banks, more institutional with less fun and less pay," he said. He certainly doesn't miss the double-dealing where a client's conversation was sometimes leaked to another potential buyer, who then came in and completed the deal. Such lack of loyalty, however, wasn't nearly as damaging as the failures prompted by creating new products (such as derivatives and mortgages) and selling them to clients who didn't understand them. He believes resulting government restrictions will continue to hamper raising intermediate capital around the world for a long time.

Reaching Out Globally

Another favorable investment career started simply enough when Ron Frasure joined Putnam Companies as a research analyst in 1970 for its mutual funds. He left Putnam in 1988 after establishing an international investing program for its clients and serving as director of asset allocation for his last five years. This international focus prompted him to start his own firm with three others. The firm was named Arcadian and was Boston-based but global in scope.

When interviewed 25 years later, Ron was proud that the firm had 190 employees and managed $50 billion in assets with clients from more than 20 countries. Less than 20% of the amount invested was in U.S. stocks. The firm follows a quantitative approach, made possible by the availability of much improved information, especially on companies in emerging markets. Ron, who retired as CEO of Arcadian at the end of 2012, traveled a lot and tailored his strategies for individual clients. "It was hard work to build something from scratch, but the experience has been very gratifying," he said. He noted that 40% of the S&P 500 profits come from non-U.S.

operations, and that there are very few companies left that are run on communist principles. "Even Vietnam is capitalist-oriented," he said.

Looking back on his busy and successful career, Ron reflects on how unpredictable and unfair life can be. He was married in 1971 and had three children, the last in 1982. Soon after that, his wife was diagnosed with Multiple Sclerosis. In 1997, she became fully incapacitated, and had to be moved to a nursing home and then into hospice care, where she died.

ADVISING FAMILY MONEY

Another 1970 grad whose initial investment job was in Boston was Jack Stewart. Jack was the first family member to go to college, and was smart enough to marry a wife who could support him when he chose to go on to graduate school. Even with her income, Jack worked at a full-time job doing research with an investment management firm in Boston during both his years at HBS.

Upon graduation, he joined the Ivy Fund doing portfolio management for two years, then moved to a small firm that was acquired by the Boston Group. While there, he worked in early stage venture capital and learned the challenges of dealing with startups. In 1980, he hopped aboard a classmate's railroad company for three years. Jack then moved back to Wellesley, Massachusetts, to help a wealthy family make private investments.

From 1983 to 1997, he worked as an employee of the family, guiding them in their stock choices, venture capital investing, and the rehabilitation of Boston buildings. When the family chose not to invest in some projects, especially small, distressed buyouts, he moved forward on his own. One was a granite company with $20 million in annual sales, which he helped turn around and then sold for a gain four years later. Another was a manufacturer of computer cabinets, which in seven years grew from $5 million to $40 million in revenue.

Jack was smart enough to sell it in 1999, a year before the tech crash ruined the business. He also was clever in buying the maintenance contracts on 20,000 water heaters from a utility and then 20,000 more on his own. These were both gas and electric water heaters installed with consumers who paid $5 per month to keep them working. When he switched to independent plumbers as subcontractors vs. union workers, his profits jumped nicely and he was bought out by another New England utility.

In 1997, Jack started his own venture capital fund, which was doing well until 1999, when he literally fell off a cliff, falling into the Grand Canyon after losing his footing. He had five operations to fix various injuries. It took three months for him to walk and three more months to walk well. Two younger people bought Jack out of the venture fund in 2000, so he had cash when the stock market ran into trouble. Jack began buying radio stations.

In 2001, he started another venture fund with classmate Carl Novotny. The fund, an SBIC (Small Business Investment Company), began with $25 million and the ability to borrow $50 million. The emphasis was investing in early-stage software. The goal was to be successful in at least 25% of the deals to help pay for those that failed.

Jack admitted that successfully finishing HBS sometimes instills arrogance in its graduates, and investing imparts a degree of humility to balance things out. "It's always good to not be the smartest guy in the room," he said, and "it helps to invest in small ponds." He personally tries to get involved with businesses "where I can be home for dinner."

LOVING LONDON

With a degree in mechanical engineering, two years in the Army, and 1½ years with Kaiser Aluminum, Don Gray came to HBS with the expectation of becoming a manager for a Fortune 500 company. During his first year, however, he enjoyed his financial courses and worked with the Putnam mutual fund company as an intern during the summer. When he graduated, he went straight into investment banking with Kidder, Peabody in New York City. He worked on many different deal financings and in 1975, at the age of 31, he was asked to run the firm's corporate finance unit in London. His main goal was to provide assistance to U.S. companies doing deals in Europe. One deal he worked on was a project financing for Iran (before the fall of the Shah) to convert flare gas into alcohol that could be shipped and later converted back to gas. As the plant was nearing completion "everyone had their hands out for payments," he said, and unqualified relatives were added to the payroll.

Although Don loved London, Morgan Stanley recruited him in 1978 to develop Morgan's eurodollar business back in the United States. There were only about 300 employees in the entire firm at the time, but after going public in 1986 it grew to nearly 50,000 employees. Don worked to help foreign companies get U.S. financing and U.S. companies to get off-shore financing if it proved less costly. For three years, he headed the investment banking unit dealing with financial institutions.

In 1990, he was ready to retire, but was persuaded instead to join UBS as its head of corporate finance in New York. He stayed for seven years until UBS was merged into another Swiss bank, after which he retired to devote himself to charitable causes. He became president of the local community fund and joined the board of the Atlantic Legal Foundation, which supported charter schools and tried to keep "junk science" out of the courtroom. He also was on the board of the organization working to combat COPD (chronic obstructive pulmonary disease).

A WINNING FORMULA

After 22 years in the investment business, Jim Parker decided to start his own firm in Houston in 1992 by farming out the back office work and hiring eight other people to work with him on the investment side. He created a screening formula that analyzes 1,500 companies to pick 50, then uses his own judgment to reduce the number to 20 and buys roughly an equal share of each. He looks primarily for mid- to high-cap growth stocks.

Jim started in New York with Channing Management, a mutual fund management firm, and three years later joined Scudder, Stevens & Clark for ten years before moving to Citicorp in Houston. Now, he does charity work and travels. He is amazed at how fast disclosures of information are now for public firms, so fast, he said, that "you can invest without leaving your seat." While the markets treated him well, he is regularly surprised by the underlying ability of the market to bounce back from adversity.

EARLY VENTURE CAPITAL

When Rick Stowe graduated in 1970, he estimates there were fewer than 200 people doing venture capital investing in the United States. "It was a club," he remembered. "The deals were syndicated since there wasn't enough money from a single firm." Rick, an electrical engineering major as an undergrad and a Baker Scholar at HBS, decided to join the club with Newcourt Securities, a $75 million venture fund that was part of the investment firm Rothschild & Company. He started in New York City and remained there for nine years, investing the firm's money in Cray Research and Federal Express, along with making other deals. He remembers the first round put into Federal Express in 1974. The round was for $4 million and gave the investors two-thirds of the company for that investment. FedEx is now worth $50 billion. As a startup, however, FedEx "was touch-and-go for a while," he said. Cray Research was equally exciting as a pioneer in showing what computers could do.

In 1979, Rick joined three others in starting a new venture firm named Welsh, Carson, Anderson & Stowe. Its focus was mainly on healthcare information and technology. Among the companies the firm invested in were Oracle, Intel, Microsoft, and Apple. Since there was limited capital for venture funds, there was also limited competition. The investments did well, and Rick retired in 1998. He stayed retired until 2001, when he joined C-B Health Ventures and became general partner of a limited partnership it started.

Rick reviewed the history of venture investing by noting that at first families did private equity investing. In the '60s, banks formed SBICs (small business investment corporations) to do early investing. In the '70s, venture funds were started and, according to Rick, "people learned as they went along." This was a time when venture capitalists (VCs) "would do any deals, but now there's specialization, at least at the larger firms." You have different people working on recruiting, operating, and financing for companies the VCs invest in. He noted that returns over the past decade have not been satisfactory, so fundraising is slowing down.

CATCHING AN INVESTMENT WAVE

Before entering HBS in the fall of 1968, Mike Terry saw the Pacific Ocean on a U.S. Navy destroyer, and spent six months off the coast of Vietnam. At HBS, he emphasized finance in his studies, and immediately after graduation put this knowledge to good use by applying for an American Express credit card that came with a $2,000 credit line. He and a classmate skipped graduation and promptly went to South America for a month of traveling before the money ran out.

Upon returning to Boston, he started his job at the Bank of Boston, where he worked for 14 years. For the first ten years, he helped grow a new business, advising smaller New England banks on how to manage their investment assets other than loans. The business grew from zero to about 130 banks under his guidance. Although an important job, the low pay caused Mike to worry about how he could afford to send his three children to college. After earning his CFA (Chartered Financial Analyst) designation in 1980, he moved into the bank's International Treasury department to manage foreign exchange trading in Europe. While still wondering about supporting the family, salvation came when he discovered he could make twice as much by moving from a bank to an investment management firm.

In 1984, he joined the firm Eaton Vance to manage taxable fixed income securities, including mutual funds and separately managed accounts. He quickly realized that if he brought in new portfolios to manage and didn't lose accounts, he would be well-rewarded. He developed a strategy emphasizing "put" bonds, which could be sold back to the issuer. He felt he had a technical advantage by being an early adopter of the specialized "Bloomberg machine" used to calculate the risks and rewards of each bond issue. He had a streak of over five years when he never had a quarter under the target index return. This out-performance enabled him to build the separate account business to over 30 accounts with about a billion dollars in total assets.

He reckons that he was lucky in what he called "catching a wave" at Eaton Vance. When he started, the firm had 40 employees and $3 billion in investment assets. When he left 17 years later, firm assets were about $70 billion. "I was working for the money, which was very good," he admitted, but when he retired he realized that the stock options he earned with the company were worth almost as much as all his salary checks combined. Even though he was paid well, Mike continued to live as though he was still getting the low pay from banking. "I have frugal genes," he explained. He bought used cars, and remained in the same house that he purchased in 1974. In 2001, he retired from Eaton Vance knowing that he had more than enough to live well for the rest of his life. He then decided he had a new job. The job description was simply, he said, "Make sure Mike has fun every day. It's the best job I ever had!"

He added, "Life is largely common sense, and I finally took myself to where the money was. I was a successful money manager, but to be honest, I've never known if I was smart or lucky, but I did keep my stupid things to a minimum." He does wonder if he should have changed jobs earlier or more often, but has no complaints about the path he took. Looking at other people and their careers, he recognizes that there "isn't a whole lot of fairness in the world." He feels that he played the career game very well for his wants and needs, and is quite happy with the way it all turned out.

12

CASHING IN

"CATCHING THE WAVE" OF GROWTH in an industry is easily the best way to have a successful business career. HBS graduates who joined financial firms, especially on Wall Street, were almost universally successful when measured by the building of wealth. While the financial markets since 1970 have had periods of downturns, overall, the stock market has gone up and attracted investment dollars from people seeking to improve their personal lives. So many investors piled in that those working in the investment area were swept upward by the momentum. New products were developed and new executive positions created to direct the money flows.

Good decisions were still essential to success. For example, banks were good but investment banks were better for personal earning power. The former emphasized stability while the latter rewarded performance. A person also had to join the right firm, especially one that was based on meritocracy and valued high ethical standards. Anyone who was greedy, however, and in a hurry for recognition often wound up failing. Those who joined the wrong firm were wise to choose another quickly.

Accepting as much responsibility as possible and pursuing diverse job assignments, even if that meant switching employers, was one way to move up. So was finding a mentor and setting high expectations both for yourself and your direct reports. From the mid-'70s to the late '80s the financial markets surged upward, sweeping everything and everyone on with it. It helped if there was a technical advantage, such as that provided by a Bloomberg machine quoting bond data. It was also a good idea not to be the smartest guy in the room, especially if you just thought you were. Financial markets have a way of humbling those who are over-confident.

Don't assume good performance will be rewarded, because there isn't a lot of fairness in the world. The best course is decision-making based on common sense, with an emphasis on keeping stupid things to a minimum. Don't argue unnecessarily with your boss, at least until you become his boss. Also, don't quit unless you have something better lined up. One classmate said only three or four major decisions during his career led him to financial success, so take the time to make sure the major decisions are right. Be careful in identifying and making such decisions, and quickly reverse course if you find yourself off-track. Try to take an equity stake in the company you work for and hold it until retirement if the firm seems to be prospering. Sometimes that stake will be worth more than the salary you earn over your employment years.

13

USING BUSINESS SKILLS IN GOVERNMENT SERVICE

T HE BUSINESS TRAINING AT HARVARD is supposed to equip graduates with a wide variety of skills. Applying these skills to government work, however, requires an individual to be especially adaptable and willing to compromise, and only a few classmates accepted the challenge.

KEEP AN EYE ON THE BIG PICTURE

One who did find success in business and government was Joe Oliver, a Canadian whose investment banking experience led to a regulatory role as executive director of the Ontario Securities Commission, and later to a seat in the Canadian Parliament. Joe had been practicing law in Montreal before leaving for HBS in 1968. At graduation, he knew that Merrill Lynch had just bought a small Canadian investment banking firm. He called Merrill Lynch and landed an investment banking position with them in New York. Because large Canadian firms were reluctant to seek assistance from an American investment bank, Joe decided to stay on but move to Toronto with Merrill. He was soon put in charge of the investment bank division and spent 12 years there helping corporate clients.

Joe took a chance in 1982 by leaving Merrill Lynch to become an equity owner in a private banking firm, investing $600,000, all of it borrowed. He was lucky when the company went public three weeks before the crash of 1987. Joe put most of the cash he received into treasury bills and suffered little damage when the market crashed. He remained with the firm until 1991, always feeling the pressure to get new investment banking business.

For two years, he ran the Ontario Securities Commission, which oversees 40% of Canadian stocks. He welcomed the chance to become involved in regulatory policy. After another two years running corporate finance for a private firm, he moved back as president of a Canadian securities trade group, which established rules of conduct. It was a self-regulatory group, but it worked with various provincial securities commissions to make capital markets both fair and efficient. He retired from this role in 2007 after 12 years. In 2008, he ran as a conservative in a liberal Toronto district with 43,000 homes and lost by 5%. He tried again and won in 2011. He was first appointed Minister of Natural Resources and in March 2014, was appointed Minister of Finance.

Whether working in the business or political world, his advice is the same: "Focus on priorities and keep an eye on the big picture. Get as many facts as you can on an issue and do a thorough analysis. Be open to the ideas from others, especially subordinates. Be flexible but never compromise your core principles. And always keep your boss in the information loop."

California Dreaming

Doing heavy lifting for Arnold Schwarzenegger doesn't seem to be a dream job, but that's what John Garamendi was asked to do when he was elected lieutenant governor of California while Arnold held the governor's spot. Fortunately for both the Republican governor and the Democratic lieutenant governor, John's position lasted a little less than three years (January 2007–November 2009) and was sandwiched between two other jobs: California Insurance Commissioner and U.S. Congressman from California's 10th District.

John went to HBS with the intent of working in the public service arena. At first, however, he took a job with Bank of America's multinational division. He found this required a lot of foreign travel, and with two young children (with four more to come), he decided after a year to try something else. He tried home building in booming California, and then became a medium-size rancher with 150 head of black Angus cattle.

At age 26, upset by both the Vietnam War and the Watergate scandal, he ran for office and was elected a state assemblyman in the California legislature, followed in 1976 by election to the state senate, where he served until 1990. He was elected California Insurance Commissioner from 1991 to 1995, served as Deputy Secretary of the Interior in the Clinton administration from 1995 to 1998, spent four years in the private sector, and then won a second term as state Insurance Commissioner (2003 to 2007).

John's dual terms leading California's insurance regulation led to significant changes. Proposition 103 regulated the price of insurance, and California went from the most expensive state for auto, home, and workers' compensation insurance to the bottom half in state listings. He tried to really understand the insurance business and to compromise with the industry when appropriate. He succeeded in smoothing the up-and-down cycles in the business for the benefit of all. He takes a dim view of handling floods and other disasters under the national insurance policy. He called it, "the Air Force One method of catastrophic coverage. The president flies in and shovels out money. It's not a good system since individuals go ahead and rebuild in the same danger areas."

John's own committee work in Congress now centers on Armed Services and Natural Resources. Going back and forth between Washington and California keeps him busy, but not so busy that he and his wife Patti can't spend time with their six children and ten grandchildren.

HONORING THE PAST

Steve Otto moved right into government work after his HBS graduation, joining the Ontario, Canada, restructuring commission, which was busy merging various departments and ministries to improve efficiency. He stayed for two years before moving to the private sector as marketing manager for a chocolate candy company. He then became manager of the firm's retail stores, staying on when LaBatt Brewing bought the company and moved the factory to downtown Toronto in the early '70s. Unfortunately, the new equipment wasn't working well, nor were the new hires who were added after the move downtown. Steve left to become managing director of a catering business serving mega-project work sites. He trimmed fat and unprofitable operations and sold the company to its employees.

In 1975, he resumed his government career, becoming executive director of Ontario's Heritage Conservation Commission, with 135 people working with him. The group managed two major historical sites in Ontario and many smaller sites. He left in 1981 to devote his full attention to Ontario's bicentennial celebration of its founding, scheduled for 1984. His title was Executive Coordinator for the Ontario government.

Since 1985, Steve has been a consultant on heritage real property, doing studies on the best use of things with historical value.

One project involved the redevelopment of 11 acres in downtown Toronto where the Hiram Walker Distillery was located. It's now a pedestrian area. He's also been writing and revising historical books about Toronto's buildings and working to preserve Fort York, Toronto's founding site.

Steve believes strongly in being involved with his community. He advised others who become involved with urban projects to "know what you're fighting for, and then go out and look for support. We need to impart values and quality into the urban fabric."

Managing Trouble

A blend of finance, real estate, and government work has filled Roslyn Braeman Payne's busy and successful business career. One of 29 women in HBS's Class of 1970, Ros went to New York City upon graduation and became a real estate investment banker. She soon learned that her MBA was not enough to become a member of the Harvard Club of NYC, which at the time didn't accept women. Recent female grads from Harvard Law School filed a lawsuit and three of her 1970 HBS classmates filed a complaint with the Human Rights Commission in New York. When it became apparent that a ruling was about to go against the club, a new vote was taken by its members. Ros and the other women were admitted beginning in 1973. The experience taught her that power is seldom willingly given, and often has to be taken.

Soon after, Ros moved to San Francisco, married, and continued to work in real estate financing. She became an officer of Genstar Corporation in the early '80s and spent her time managing real estate enterprises and reorganizing various real estate joint ventures. Ros's varied experiences in real estate led to a job as President of the Federal Asset Disposition Association, the predecessor of the Resolution Trust Corporation. Her job as president, from 1986 to 1988, was to direct 400 employees at the government-sponsored

181

organization, which advised saving and loan financial companies on how to get troubled real estate loans repaid. Success was judged by how much and how fast money was recovered.

In 1988, with two growing sons, she founded the private investment firm Jackson Street Partners. Ros led this firm into private equity and emerging markets while diversifying out of real estate. She also joined the board of First America Corporation, where she served from 1988 to 2009.

In looking back at her career, Ros observed that human behavior is often greedy and can cause problems for everyone. Before taking on any task, she advised making sure the culture of the organization aligns well with your own personal views. In one new task she was asked to take on, she found that her HBS education, and work experience with capital leverage and business management, were critical elements in arranging a successful collaboration between HBS and the Harvard School of Public Health.

PROMOTING CAPITALISM

For 25 years, Austin Belton worked in the financial world of mutual funds, money management, and corporate finance before moving to Washington, D.C. to join OPIC, a U.S. government-controlled corporation handling project financing and investment in private companies in Africa, Russia, Eastern Europe, and Latin America. "Our job was to introduce capitalism to these areas and encourage the formation of private investment partnerships, usually with one-third private equity and two-thirds debt," he said.

Austin came to HBS after earning a law degree, spending three years in the Navy, and practicing law for 2½ years in New York City. Between his first and second years of the MBA program, he went to Geneva, Switzerland, to help Bernie Cornfeld sell off-shore mutual funds. The company was Investors Overseas Service (IOS) and Austin's work, as a lawyer, helped get around foreign exchange restrictions that were hindering investment in international mutual funds. The thought was good, but Cornfeld was accused of stealing money from the company, which later filed for bankruptcy. Fortunately, Austin had been advised not to rejoin his summer employer, so avoided the negative stigma connected with IOS.

Instead, upon graduation, Austin joined the blue chip financial partnership Brown Brothers Harriman and stayed for 25 years. In his early years, he handled corporate workouts and troubled financial deals. Later, he did lending and corporate finance work, establishing, according to him, "tremendous overseas relationships" along the way. For example, he helped DuPont and GM on exchange rates, moved German money into the coffee business in Central and South America, and even helped Norwegian salmon farmers set up an operation in Maine.

After three years working for the U.S. government-owned OPIC, he moved to the InterAmerican Development Bank, an international organization funded by various national governments, including the United States. This entity raised private funds to invest in big infrastructure projects in Central America and also in various foreign companies. Private funds were raised via ten-year partnerships, with the expectation that the initial losses would be offset by later profits and a reasonable return would accrue to investors. The desire to lend proved stronger than the focus on sound investments, and the program struggled. Austin moved on to the U.S. Small Business Administration, where both public and private funds were raised to help finance, with grants and loans, companies in the inner city and low income areas throughout the United States.

Austin was with the SBA for three years and then joined the Asian Development Bank in Manila, which again provided financing to areas, especially in the Philippines, where traditional bank financing was difficult to obtain. This effort also had its problems, especially in some countries where money given to a person or entity was delivered a few days later to somewhere else. "You have to be vigilant to avoid the bad guys," Austin advised.

How successful these financing programs have been "cannot accurately be measured on an annual basis, especially since success may take ten years," he said. "You also can't expect that corporate accounting systems for the government will be realistic."

BEING A BANKER

The career path after HBS for Warren Luke was pretty clear when he arrived at the school in 1968. Warren's ancestors came from China to Hawaii in the 1870s and his father had founded the successful Hawaii National Bank in Honolulu in 1960. Warren was destined to join the family business, which included the bank, real estate development, property management, and insurance.

The bank is now 99.5% controlled by Warren's family, and even with over $500 million in assets, describes itself as a community bank helping locally owned businesses, primarily those involved in Hawaiian real estate. With the bank so locally focused and conservatively run, Warren has devoted himself to numerous nonprofit activities. He's been on the boards of the San Francisco Federal Reserve, the U.S. Red Cross, Babson College (Boston), the Punahou School (the largest public high school in Honolulu), and has served as Treasurer of the United Way of America (the D.C.-based governing body of local United Ways in the United States). For the Punahou School, which educated both president Obama and the former president of China, he developed a two-week program in Honolulu to provide leadership training to 30 high school leaders annually from both the United States and China.

Warren said he meets a lot of interesting people while on public service boards. He also believes nonprofits open opportunities for other business. All this service work does have one downside: halfway through 2015, he had already flown more than 100,000 miles.

Lucky for him, he has four children, three with Harvard MBAs, ready to assist in the family business.

REAL ESTATE REALITY

A public/private career for Andy Barnes began when he took his first job as assistant to the president of Boise Cascade and met Ralph Nader, who at the time was pushing environmental responsibility for real estate developers. He described Nader as "an extreme person who put his finger on some real problems," and was impressed by his dedication to a cause. Andy stayed with Boise for 3½ years, part of the time serving as project manager for Incline Village, a building project on Lake Tahoe.

He moved on to join the Rouse Company as it was developing Columbia, Maryland, which he described as the "latest and greatest" example of the perfect city. The effort, hurt by the recession in 1974, proved only partially successful in providing an ideal middle class living center. He then was chosen from 3,000 applicants to become one of 15 White House Fellows. Among his assignments was working on arms control for the State Department.

When he finished his one-year stint at the White House, he met the chairman of the Pennsylvania Avenue Development Company, which was then rebuilding an area of 25 city blocks in downtown D.C., which had been red-lined by the banks and got no loans. He was hired as CEO of the effort, with a staff of 60. Over the next four years, he attracted $500 million of new investment into the area, including a new Marriott hotel, The National Theatre, and the office of a major law firm.

Andy moved back to private business by joining a real estate asset management firm in San Francisco as a managing partner. After four years, he co-founded a firm investing in real estate, selling out to his partner in 1992. At age 49, he moved to Paris, living there for a year before spending time in Prague and Moscow. When he returned, he joined the San Francisco Planning and Urban Research Group, which sought to minimize the environmental impact of area building projects. He soon became chairman of the organization, serving for three years. Denver then called on him to use his expertise to redevelop 4,400 acres owned by the city as part of the Stapleton Development Corporation.

In 1998, Andy went back to San Francisco to establish his own firm advising landowners and others on how to optimize land use. He now spends about one-third of his time working for nonprofits and two-thirds of his time working for profit. He emphasized that his learning at HBS was not just about business. "The school taught us to be critical thinkers and to develop organizational and leadership skills." He's applied this learning in a variety of situations during his career.

TAKE AN EARLY RISK

One member of the Class of 1970 who asked not to be named spent 18 years consulting for small and medium business firms and nine more years working for a book company before moving to a governmental role in advising family businesses. "I wish I had known myself better," he said. "I would have taken the risk earlier of moving into politics." This individual still coaches small businesses. He observed that "entrepreneurs lack management experience but wind up leading organizations despite that lack."

14

BLENDING A BUSINESS/ GOVERNMENT CAREER

WHILE IT MIGHT SEEM NATURAL for the well-trained business person to use skills for personal profit in the corporate world and also for serving in government in the nonprofit world, it doesn't happen often. One person who was interviewed explained that while working in government used to be a badge of honor, it's become a lightning rod for criticism. Business approaches are not necessarily welcomed by politicians or their constituents. Tough decisions are avoided or postponed rather than dealt with. Added scrutiny comes to the outsider who tries to help, with hidden motives assumed until proven otherwise. For many successful business people, working in Washington, D.C., or with any government entity, is more of a hassle than it's worth.

For those who do accept the challenge of working in government, special skills are needed including the ability to accept criticism, hear different views from others, and compromise one's own positions. So, too, is accepting less-than-perfect results that come from trying to reach a general agreement with multiple parties. These are also traits that might frustrate a hard-driving business leader. Going from business to government and back again can also be disorienting. Do you want to reach quick decisions, or can you spend the time reaching a consensus?

For those taking on government-related responsibilities, it's important that the culture of the organization aligns with your personal views. For example, it's noble to lend money to Third-World and inner-city projects that could improve their citizens' futures. If, however, the money given flows elsewhere or becomes an avenue to personal enrichment, the effort may have a net negative result. Doing the right thing is not necessarily easy despite the best intentions.

15

SWITCHING CAREERS

T HE SHIFTING SANDS OF TIME prompt changes for everyone, HBS grads included. Many classmates moved in one direction for a career path and found it not to their liking. Or perhaps they found a career more suitable for their personal interests. In any case, changes that were made were often surprising and abrupt. These included: at least two students who left banking to train for the priesthood; one who traded business consulting for a career in magic; a well-educated woman who abandoned an investment career for life as an author/artist; another woman who left a high-powered corporate track to become a professional photographer; and five who held various corporate jobs before moving into the field of executive recruiting. Many more switched from careers with high financial rewards to careers offering high levels of personal satisfaction. One of the best things about holding an HBS MBA is the freedom it gives graduates to make such choices.

THE BANKER PRIEST

Rod Quainton became an Episcopal priest after 15 years in commercial banking. He began his career as one of 39 MBAs hired in 1970 to be commercial bankers at the First National Bank of Chicago, which was pushing hard to grow its lending business. A fast pace and demanding leadership shrunk the 39 number down to only 13 in two years. Rod stayed on. His early years were spent in the troubled industries of airlines and aerospace, and he wound up on creditor committees when four of his clients, Lockheed, TWA, Pan Am, and Eastern, went into bankruptcy reorganization.

After that experience, he welcomed the opportunity to move on, and in 1976, First Chicago named him deputy general manager of its Tokyo branch in Japan. "I learned to listen," he remembered. "Silence is part of the negotiating process." While he was in Tokyo, a Japanese woman employee committed suicide. He attended her Buddhist funeral. After lighting incense, he made the sign of the cross. Japanese coworkers thanked him for the Christian blessing.

In 1979, he moved again, this time to New York City to handle loan accounts for ten of the largest U.S. companies, including General Motors. Reasoning that you "have to go behind the scenes to really know the customer," he toured GM's Tarrytown plant, where the "J" car was being built. He contrasted the dirty and slow GM production line with his tour of a Mazda plant making cars with Wankel engines in Hiroshima, Japan. The Mazda plant was efficient and so clean "you could eat off the floor," he said. He was not surprised as Japanese cars moved strongly into the U.S. market.

In 1982, he was assigned to be regional manager for First Chicago's Houston office, where he stayed for three years feeling more and more like a corporate nomad. His wife had suggested finding friends at the local church. Rod taught Bible study classes and found several men coming to him for advice and counseling. When his wife suggested he might be happier if he became an Episcopal priest, he cashed in his retirement savings and, at the age of 45, went to seminary school for three years in Austin, Texas. As a side job, he taught finance and business ethics to business school seniors at the University of Texas. Students began coming to him to talk about their lives. He also served on the board of a nonprofit organization helping the poor and homeless by offering job counseling, shelter, food, clothes, and medical assistance.

A two-year stint in Fort Lauderdale as a priest was followed by three years in Abilene, Texas, where he was with a large church in a small town. The regular relocating and Rod's devotion to his new work took a toll on his marriage, and after 25 years, he and his wife divorced. "I'd taken the church as a mistress," he admitted. He moved again in 1995, this time back to Chicago, where he brought senior clergy and business leaders together to discuss ethics and values. Four years later, he was asked to join the First United Methodist Church in Birmingham, Michigan, as director of adult education. He also offered counsel to unemployed autoworkers in the area. Rod's advice to others: "Don't follow the money. Follow the passion. Know who you are and where you can help."

TEACHING ETHICS

Rick Shreve offers similar advice to business grads: "Live your life in a way that you can look back and feel good about what you've done 40 years from now." Rick followed his own wisdom by building a comfortable nest egg during 18 years as an investment banker at Morgan Stanley. He then spent three years earning a master of divinity degree from Yale University. Since he wasn't able to convince himself he was suitable for priesthood, he and his wife and five adopted children moved to Hanover, New Hampshire, where he worked as a lay chaplain for the hospital and joined the faculty at Dartmouth's Tuck School of Business as adjunct professor of business ethics.

Rick had come to HBS as a lieutenant commander in the Navy after seven years on submarines, once spending "an entire year of my life underwater." He interviewed at HBS in his full uniform, as he came straight off the submarine to the campus interview. Between his two years at HBS, he worked a summer job for Morgan Stanley, initially wondering, what's an investment banker? When he joined the firm full-time, his assignment was building relationships with clients, but this job evolved into a situation where transaction fees mattered most. Morgan grew rapidly and then went public. Rick had to hold his stock for two years before he could cash out in 1988, but this was a profitable two years. He recalled that "leaving Morgan Stanley was the worst financial thing I've done, but overall it was the best thing I've ever done."

"I've had a pretty good run. I had some success in business and I hope I've done some good." He views teaching ethics as a kind of ministry, and he enjoys it. He quotes Aristotle, who said, "You are defined by your actions." Rick believes most people in business are decent people trying to do the right thing, but significant business moves often involve ethical dilemmas. He enjoys helping his students anticipate and resolve such dilemmas.

It's Magic

Guy Camirand's career was also divided into two parts: first as a businessman/consultant and later as a professional magician. Guy started to study magic in Quebec City at age 11, and performed shows while he earned an electrical engineering degree from Laval University in Montreal and finished his studies at HBS. He held six jobs during the '70s, all business-related in Canada, and joined the Canadian government in 1983 to help reverse $100 million in losses at a government-owned steel mill and at iron ore mines. He succeeded by shutting one mine, transferring half the workers to the second mine, "and making an entire town disappear" by buying houses from the moving mine workers and returning the area to wilderness.

Guy describes himself as a workaholic, and the open-ended jobs in consulting occupied his time and hurt his marriage. In 1990, he divorced his wife ("on a friendly basis") and decided to pursue his real love—magic. He remembers living very inexpensively from 1990 to 2000. He also wrote books (seven short booklets in the "Master of Magic" series), performed magic in Quebec and at various conventions, taught two magic courses at Laval University, created new tricks and videos, and grew the Camirand Academy of Magic, which he had established with Gary Ouellet in 1978.

Guy takes his magic seriously. He has taken classes in clown skills, dancing, speech, mime, and drama, all to help himself as a magician. He explained, "Magic doesn't entertain, the performer does. I try to create the impossible, and bring laughter to the audience." He puts little emphasis on gadgets, but his high-end products and innovative reputation help him make a good living. Even so, he emphasized that "success is not necessarily measured in terms of wealth."

ENTREPRENEUR TO EDUCATOR

The first 27 years of Jim Ellis's career were devoted to retail business in southern California, initially as an employee but later as a serial entrepreneur with various firms selling consumer products. In 1996, he was at a Young Presidents Organization (YPO) meeting when, in a group discussion, he was challenged to think how he wanted to spend the next 25 years of his life. He decided he wanted something different, and his wife agreed. He considered writing a book, consulting, or delivering paid speeches, but decided to give teaching a try when the University of Southern California offered him a position. He initiated the sale of three businesses he was running at the time and moved into the classroom.

Jim discovered he had a great passion for teaching. He always found time to talk with his students, and he was well-liked for his extra efforts. In 2007, after ten years of teaching, he became dean of USC's business school, the Marshall School of Business. He was one of only two deans at the top 25 U.S. business schools who didn't hold a doctorate degree. He found the job, as he said, "more time-consuming than anything I've ever done." He took responsibility for 3,700 business majors, 900 business minors, 1,700 MBA students, and 82 Ph.D. candidates. In 2012, he was signed to a second five-year contract.

In comparing life as an entrepreneur vs. an academic, he said the former has to "think differently, take risks, and be creative." His early business experience, however, also helped him prepare for academic life, which requires "a sense of urgency, attention to detail, and the ability to treat customers (the students) as most important."

SMART & UNCONVENTIONAL

Reba White Williams almost certainly became the most educated member of Harvard Business School's Class of 1970. She finished college at Duke, got her MBA from Harvard, received a master's in art history at Hunter College, a doctorate in art history at City University of New York, and a master's in fiction writing from Antioch College. Her business training began in 1959 at McKinsey Consulting, where she was a researcher for nine years before attending HBS. She then worked as a securities analyst on Wall Street for five years and wrote and did research for *Institutional Investor* magazine for three years after that.

Reba credits Tony Athos for persuading her to seek an MBA, noting that at the time, he was the HBS professor charged with assembling the Class of 1970 and also was a consultant for McKinsey. "Tony was interested in having a very different and exciting class. He wanted to bring smart but unconventional students together."

Reba's husband, also an HBS grad, became CEO of Alliance Capital. Her hobby of collecting prints and desire to meet different types of people moved her into the business of dealing with prints made by American artists. She became president of the New York City Art Commission and vice chairman of the New York State Council of the Arts. Her art collection allowed her to donate about 5,000 prints to the National Gallery of Art in Washington, D.C. In her spare time, she has also completed three books of fiction: "Restrike" (2013), "Fatal Impressions" (2014), and "Angels" (2014).

Her advice is a reflection of her own life: "Try to exercise and broaden your mind. Keep trying new things. Take a course and learn something new. Don't let yourself be too narrow. Follow this advice and you'll keep more alive."

SWITCHING EMPHASIS

B. J. Krintzman entered HBS at age 21, which she said made her the youngest person in the Class of 1970. She switched emphasis numerous times: from housewife to nonprofits to law and to broker arbitration, supporting herself as a single parent. She got married between her first and second years, and worked only summer jobs and wrote an investment newsletter before starting a family. Sons were born in 1972 and 1975 and she remained out of the workforce.

In 1979, she was divorced and went on 17 job interviews. One executive interviewing her asked, "What will you do when your children get sick?" She eventually took a job as managing director of the Boston Shakespeare Company and later spent three years as director of planning for the Boston Symphony Orchestra. Raising her sons and work as a real estate broker kept her busy, but she found time to earn a law degree in 1991.

For nearly four years, she worked at the large Boston law firm of Hale & Dorr, mainly doing employment and domestic relations work. She left to work on her own from an office in her Newton,

Massachusetts, home. She called working with different attorneys "eye-opening." She frequently saw big, powerful law firms utilize what she called a "scorched earth philosophy" to win a case.

While on her own, she took an arbitration case, and decided to study and become a full-time arbitrator/mediator. Her work now involves settling disputes between brokers and their clients on security purchases, and between brokers and broker-dealers on employment cases. "When the market goes down, cases go up," she observed. Now she spends about 20% of her time doing arbitration and denies that the "little guy" always get the short stick. "Since 2008 I've ruled for tens of millions of dollars against brokerage firms," she said.

STEPPING OFF THE CORPORATE LADDER

As a Harvard College graduate who became an employee at HBS grading business policy papers written by second-year students, Candace Gaudiani was familiar with the school when she was accepted into the Class of 1970. She earned her MBA and went to work for an advertising firm, but soon joined Cleveland-based Cole National. She was assigned to the "Can-Do Shops," later renamed "Things Remembered" for various name- engraved items given as gifts. She helped grow the unit from one store to 110 stores with 450 employees. After three years, however, a new merchandising manager was hired and new directions were set. Candace left to join McKinsey Consulting.

Candace was married to a doctor and worked long hours for McKinsey in both Cleveland and Washington, D.C., from 1973 to 1977. In 1976, she had a baby, the first woman consultant at McKinsey to do so and continue working. For the next two years, she was a full-time McKinsey team member, with McKinsey allowing her to work exclusively on "in-town" studies to permit her to raise her daughter. Officially, she was paid as an outside consultant.

In 1979, she joined FMC and was assigned to work with the Bradley Fighting Vehicle production division. She helped build a team of 50 people, tested the vehicle in the Nevada desert, and spent much of her time introducing cost control methods to the U.S. Army. She also had daughters #2 and #3. At age 41, busy at home with three girls, Candace stepped off the corporate ladder and began a successful period on her own investing in public companies and a few startups. With her daughters launched and eventually on their way to Harvard, she moved her career to, what she called, "photography as art," and now sells her work professionally.

Having a family and pursuing a corporate career at the same time is not easy but can be done. She advised, "You have to be fully engaged in whatever you do, and give it everything you've got. Always be of value, be ethical, do what you love to do, and treasure friendships." Candace and her female classmates represent less than 4% of the Class of 1970. Now, women at HBS comprise 42% of the enrollment.

EXECUTIVE RECRUITING

At least five classmates spent five to 15 years gathering corporate experiences and then shifted to the relatively new and rapidly expanding field of executive recruiting. These classmates had varied business experiences, were quick to understand job requirements, had the confidence to deal with top corporate executives, and had a built-in network of contacts courtesy of HBS alumni associations. They also had the benefits gained from many case study discussions in the classroom, where valuing other viewpoints was the key to success.

Len Pfeiffer expected to be in the Army after going through ROTC training in college at Harvard, but a failed physical ended that path and he moved across the Charles River to pursue an MBA. Like many HBS graduates who entered straight from college, the summer of 1970 was used to ease back. In Len's case, he jumped into his Pontiac GTO and drove across the country from June to September, stopping to work odd jobs when money ran low.

In October, 1970, he joined American Express as an internal consultant. With little cooperation amongst the various business units, he found gathering information was best done by posing as a student from Columbia University rather than admitting he was an employee. He watched as people competed internally rather than externally, and realized "you're only as good as your last big deal." After brief stints with Amex's "Space Bank" (a hotels.com-type business that was too far ahead of the curve) and a marketing slot in the credit card group, he decided to move on.

He briefly worked in London for Simplified Travel, but that firm went under. He took over the company's Pan Am account, promoting the sale of discount books for hotels and restaurants. When it came time to collect the $5,000 fee due him, Pan Am refused payment saying Len's contract was "not in writing." An expensive lesson learned.

At this point, his career was interrupted by a personal tragedy. Len was leaving his ground floor apartment in New York City when a girl in the neighboring apartment asked if she could put some food in his refrigerator. Len said "sure" and left to run an errand. When he returned, his apartment door was open and as he walked inside he found an intruder who held a butcher knife to the girl's throat and threatened to kill her. Len charged and wrestled the intruder and managed to push him out the door. In the fight, Len had grabbed the knife's blade and sliced his right hand almost completely off. The girl was frightened but uninjured and Len spent 12 hours in surgery, six days in the hospital, and a year regaining feeling in his right hand.

Later in 1974, he joined an executive recruiting firm on Wall Street. In 1978, Korn Ferry, another executive recruiting firm, hired him away. For the next 20 years, Len worked for them, first in New York and then in Washington, D.C., after becoming the firm's youngest partner. When internal politics began to hinder the company's progress, Len moved to rival executive recruiting firm Heidrick & Struggles (H&S). Company-wide disenchantment and significant turnover at his new employer prompted another change. In 2001, he started his own business in Washington by emphasizing senior executive recruitment for nonprofits and trade organizations. It was a gutsy move since at the time he was 54, had a non-working wife, and four children.

Len is both successful and happy with his own firm and expects to continue working at least for a few more years. Looking back at what he'd do differently, he lists three things: "I'd be bolder and more self-confident, not assuming that an older person is any wiser. I'd spend more time developing relationships with people. I never really worked my Harvard connections. Finally, I'd try to balance my life a little more and avoid those 70- to 80-hour work weeks."

STAYING IN BOSTON

Bob Hallagan, an All-American lacrosse player who worked at Citibank prior to coming to HBS, wanted to stay in the Boston area after graduation. He was recommended by two classmates for a position as assistant to the president of the Boston Stock Exchange. He took it and was quickly promoted to CFO and then COO, remaining with the Exchange for five years. He next joined a small brokerage firm as a trader, but two years later, the firm was sold to a large investment firm and Bob was asked to move to New York City.

He remained in Boston by joining Heidrick & Struggles in 1977, thinking he had signed on for a year. Instead he stayed on, serving two three-year terms as CEO beginning in 1990. With the exception of a brief time in Washington, D.C., to run the Center for Board Leadership (a joint venture between H&S and the Association for Corporate

Directors), Bob remained for 30 years and helped H&S go public in 1998. In 2007, he moved to another recruiting firm, Korn Ferry. He spends a lot of time on airplanes and primarily recruits board members for Fortune 500 companies. "I keep doing it because it keeps me sharp," he explained.

When asked what he looks for in top executives, he says he wants candidates who are thrown into "stretch" jobs early in their careers and are focused and work hard. He said, "The best people are already enormously successful in business and have a vision as to where every job assignment leads. Don't get too narrowly trained," he warned. He also doesn't favor those working with startup businesses. These companies generally fail, and the recruiters are looking for successes.

When seeking board members for major companies, he wants to see good decision-making and success in their own careers. "You look for the ability to attract top talent and for people with impeccable ethics and integrity," he said. With directors more responsible to shareholders now, "you even get down to a candidate's personal life, which is sometimes ignored in the race to the top. Happy people have a happy family life, are healthy, and stay relevant."

HEADING DOWN UNDER

David Pumphrey took an unusual route in getting to HBS. A native of Britain, he had already completed a year of higher education and case studies at the Cranfield School of Management. This school, 90 minutes north of London, had an understanding that if Cranfield's graduates were accepted at HBS, they would skip the first-year program and enter as second-year students. This David did after spending the summer of 1969 working for McKinsey Consulting in London. He was one of six Cranfield grads who came to HBS in 1969.

In 1970, with a freshly printed MBA, he returned to McKinsey in London. He stayed for two years and then joined a venture capital firm. He was assigned to one of the firm's portfolio companies, a small toy manufacturer, with instructions to make it grow. This he did via acquisitions over a four-year period. Later, he was sent to a struggling manufacturing company that was in the portfolio, and managed to sell that firm.

It was 1981, and at the urging of HBS classmates who had returned to their native Australia, David convinced his wife to join him in moving "down under." After first doing some venture capital work, he signed on as an executive recruiter with Spencer Stuart's Sydney office. In 1993, he joined Heidrick & Struggles to do similar executive searches, especially in the education and social enterprise areas. His work took him to Russia, the Asia-Pacific area, the United Kingdom, and America, but he remained headquartered in Sydney until semi-retirement in 2012.

When asked to comment on changes in the executive recruiting business, David said it has become very competitive with firms trying to build relationships with customer companies by going beyond single searches. They work with the companies to identify internal candidates as potential leaders and make sure their work experiences prepare them for top positions. Sometimes company boards neglect identifying future needs and preparing candidates for success. He estimates that 90% of all top people at major companies now are hired with the help of executive search firms.

The typical CEO candidate is over 35 years, has a successful track record that has been recognized, and has a deep network of contacts within an industry. One of the most important search functions is confirming "realities" on a resume: educational background, job experiences, etc. Although rare, any sign of deception quickly disqualifies a candidate. Helping the screening process are

"360-degree reviews," where not just a boss is asked for references but also peers, subordinates, competitors, etc.

RECRUITING FOR TECHNOLOGY

The military had first call on the talents of Dave Francis, but injuries ruined two opportunities to serve. Dave said he couldn't afford an Ivy League education when he graduated from high school. Instead, he accepted a free education at West Point, graduating in 1962. A shoulder injury from playing football kept him from going to Vietnam, so he went into pilot training with the Air Force and completed the program in 1967. A final physical, however, showed he had suffered a heart attack previously, thus grounding him as a pilot. With military options limited, he joined a small West Coast electronics firm before applying to HBS.

After leaving Harvard in 1970, Dave chose to go back to his previous employer, the electronics firm, rather than join a large firm. This job only lasted two years before GE recruited him into a new technical ventures group, which would develop new companies from research spun out of GE. He did this for six years and started eight new companies. He felt, however, that the effort wasn't working because GE would only let its research be spun out to a separate company if the research didn't show much promise. The new companies were thus "resurrection" situations, forced to seek outside capital if they were to survive.

Dave resigned from this position, but CEO Jack Welch persuaded him to work on the consumer finance side of GE as an alternative. He became head of GE's private label credit card business with 3,000 people under his direction. He later was asked to work in Europe with GE's plastics division. Two small daughters prompted him to decline this opportunity and to leave GE.

In 1981, Heidrick & Struggles in New York City wanted him to help find people to work with big companies. He said he'd join only if he could recruit for smaller companies and venture capital firms, and establish a technology practice. Over the next 20 years, his firm went from $60 million in total revenues to $620 million, with technology accounting for $240 million of that.

For Dave, the end to this string of growth came when the internet bubble burst in 2001–2002. Revenues for executive recruiting firms dropped to half of what they had been. Dave called it "two years of hell" and watched as H&S stock went from a $14 per share value in 1999 to $75 in 2000 and then $12 in 2002. Competition from LinkedIn and Monster.com provided further competitive challenges.

Dave and three partners left H&S to start their own firm, but Dave had to step aside when a tumor affected his hearing nerve and his balance. Surgery was successful in helping Dave recover most of his balance, but it did cause complete hearing loss in one ear. He was unable to drive and urged not to fly in an airplane, so Dave retired from executive recruiting.

Dave reflected on how people pursue business careers. He estimated that 90% of people seeking work "fall into things because other people decide the path for them," even if it means they do things they really don't want to do. Others make profitable career moves only if they sacrifice their family situations, are willing to rise to the top on the backs of others, suffer multiple divorces, neglect their children, etc. He recommended "reaching the pinnacle of success on your own terms," noting that even billionaires can have unhappy lives.

He further observed that "executive success depends on the stage of the company's growth and the general culture. An entrepreneur successful in starting a company usually isn't successful in growing one."

A WEALTH OF EXPERIENCES

John Gardner spent just over 15 years working in various positions before being hired by the executive recruiting firm Lamalie to work in its Chicago office. John began his career with merchandisers Federated and Cole National, and afterwards moved to McKinsey for five years to help clients develop marketing strategies. American Optical recruited him to handle strategic planning, and subsequently put him in charge of its medical instrument business. He left after three years when a new CEO was brought in. He spent 1½ years at Foto Mart as SVP of marketing, then joined GE's lighting group as head of strategic planning where he remained for four years.

He spent six years at Lamalie before being recruited by competitor Heidrick & Struggles, where he remained for 20 more years and became vice chairman as the firm expanded to 450 consultants and more than 2,500 employees. "I regret that I didn't find the right thing for me earlier, but if I had, I wouldn't have had the wealth of experiences I enjoyed," John commented.

When asked what he looked for in recruiting CEOs, John mentions relevant experience and integrity. He also said "cultural fit" was important, noting that values and style in a company have to match up with the candidate. He cited as an example being frugal or extravagant. Finally, he looks for people with broad experiences who would be able to make the step up to CEO if they weren't already holding such a title. He cautioned that problems might be created if a retiring CEO makes the selection of his successor, usually choosing a loyalist or someone similar in image to the departing CEO.

John and his wife are doing a lot of traveling now, joining five other H&S alumni couples on cruises when they can. "It's about family and friends, not excelling at business. You don't win by being smartest, but by being somebody who's honest and respected."

LOYALTY TO A POINT
In the fast-changing world of banking, Tom Gaspard had the unusual resume of being with the same employer for over 30 years. "It was a great choice," Tom said of joining Citibank in New York City

after graduation. He wanted a line position working as a decision-maker directly responsible for making a profit. Instead, he was put into the bank's operations area processing bank transactions. In six months, he had 150 people working for him, but without profit-making responsibility.

He moved into running branches in New York City, then to Washington, D.C., where he became local CEO for Citibank's unit there. In the early '90s, he was called back to New York to head up one of ten internal trouble-shooting task forces working with CEO John Reid. Next, he was sent to Santa Monica, California, to be head of the bank's transaction technology program. A 1999 transfer brought him back to New York in the consumer investment group.

This path came to an abrupt end in 2001 when Travelers, the large insurance and investment brokerage firm run by Sandy Weil, bought Citibank. The cultural and salary structure of the investment bank didn't mesh well with a commercial bank. Ethical problems and cronyism created further friction, he said. Tom accepted a buyout package and departed.

Tom next tried residential real estate development in Delaware. By 2005, he concluded that there was more supply than demand, and the only thing that could make the numbers work was continued escalation of home values, which to him was not a certainty. He left the business.

A friend steered him to the private fiduciary business where, for an hourly fee, he helps choose money managers and handles trust administration. He frequently works with estate attorneys, but believes a situation where the attorney is also the trustee results in a conflict of interest. He commented, "I have to be detail oriented and show personal attention, being responsive to the client. I can't delegate decisions to a back-up."

Looking back at his Citibank career, two lessons were most remembered. First, in 1981, online banking was introduced, but customers didn't want it. "Sometimes you can be too far in front to succeed," he said. Second, initially Citibank relied on mortgage brokers to send it business. "These brokers were primarily used by those with credit problems." When the bank moved to make its own direct mortgages, he noticed, "The difference in quality was like night and day. You need to trust but verify, and have to be careful offering volume incentives even to your own employees."

THREE CAREER PATHS

Three widely different career experiences were enjoyed by Bob Gibb after he left HBS: 1) working for one of the premier technical companies as it grew rapidly; 2) joining his family farming business in Manitoba, Canada; and 3) starting an investment firm dedicated to buying small companies and helping them grow.

Raychem was Bob's first employer. It was a material science company with products in telecommunications, electronics, and the industrial defense industry. He worked first in the company's California headquarters and then became an industrial sales engineer in Chicago. After five years, his family needed him to help run its 14,000-acre farm outside Winnipeg. He stayed for six years and discovered, according to Bob, there "was too much risk relative to the rewards available" for him to remain. The farm raised corn for use in a whisky distillery, but it was sold when interest rates rose to high levels and the distillery was closed.

Raychem invited Bob to rejoin them in Toronto as president of Canadian operations. He accepted and remained for eight years before being recruited to help British-Oxygen integrate its Canadian and U.S. operations. Bob stayed on for three years after the French firm Air Liquide bought the operation, but then decided he would run his own operation.

In 1996, he started the Cypress Group, a family investment firm buying companies with less than $50 million in revenues. The firm bought six companies, including a fertilizer business, a medical distribution operation, a software company, and an engineered-fabrics business for medical and technology uses. He grew them successfully by choosing companies with good management and an ability to manage risks. Bob enjoys this last supervisory role most of all. "The beauty of this is I manage my own time," he said.

CONSULTANT TO TEACHER

Barry Hedley has given a lot of advice to clients during his 27 years as a consultant, but he now passes his wisdom on to students at the University of Cambridge's business school in England. He has a lot of stories to tell. He first spent six years with the Boston Consulting Group and worked for three years at various manufacturing companies. Later, he formed his own consulting firm, which he built into an international powerhouse.

His Braxton Associates was started in 1979 in Europe with an emphasis on international strategy. The firm grew to 125 people before being bought in 1984 by the accounting firm Touche Ross, which in turn was combined with Deloitte. Barry, a Baker Scholar at HBS, then directed the growth of Deloitte Consulting, establishing 20 offices with over 1,000 employees and $4 billion in revenue worldwide. He retired in 2000. When the consulting operation separated from the accounting part of Deloitte in 2002, it went back to using the Braxton name.

Barry mentions that the total endowment of Cambridge and its colleges is less than the annual return on Harvard's endowment. To help improve the finances, he's introduced networking and modeled fundraising on the Harvard model. In teaching, he encourages "the power of teams" with the thought that everyone can contribute if they are listened to, recognized, and encouraged. His motto is "no problem is too difficult, and no responsibility too large." He suggested taking a big picture look at situations, and warned not to strive for too much precision.

ON THE ROAD AGAIN

"Management consulting is a good job for young people, but if you're married and have children, it's difficult to be a consultant." So said Alan Minoff, who spent 16 years as a consultant before abandoning the vagabond lifestyle and international travel for a corporate job with a large retailer.

Al got a taste for travel after graduation, when he boarded a Boston-London charter flight, bought a VW camper for European delivery, and wandered European campgrounds for ten weeks before returning to the United States. "I had no money or assets, but could borrow on my HBS degree," he explained. When he returned, he got a job at the Boston Consulting Group. He worked at BCG, which in 1970 had only 25 employees, for nine years. He traveled extensively advising on pricing strategies and helping firms determine overall corporate strategy. He joined Management Analysis Center in Chicago next, doing much the same type of consulting for seven years, working primarily in South America.

After 16 years in the consulting business, he was tired of traveling and being away from his family despite the interesting and challenging projects he had worked on. He joined Sears in Chicago as VP of mergers and acquisitions with the goal of acquiring specialty retailers. After new management took over at Sears and closed his division, he stayed on at Sears working on special projects for a couple years before retiring.

Alan advised not to bother getting an MBA unless you get into one of the top five or six business schools in the country. He praised the HBS alumni network, which helped him when traveling or needing advice. "I went to the HBS database and people would take my call." Other business schools also promote their alumni networks. But HBS has longer and stronger bonds than most, and these stretch worldwide. The Cleveland HBS Club, for example, has over 150 dues-paying members and 15–20 programs per year.

There are more than 100 HBS clubs and associations worldwide, including Beijing, Israel, Brazil, India, Thailand, Japan, Nigeria, Peru, Greece, and Iceland.

CHOOSING FAMILY OVER CORPORATE

Cummins Corporation, the company famous for making truck engines, gave Robert Berman a $3,000-per-year grant to attend Harvard Business School. When Robert finished school, he was not ready to return to Cummins in Columbus, Indiana, so instead, he went to Switzerland as a case-writer for IMEDE, an international business school started by Nestle to train its management and others. In 1971, he rejoined Cummins as director of planning for the engine business, and was moved to London to open sales offices in Europe. When he was brought back to the United States, he went to Dallas as the president of the Cummins' subsidiary Fleetguard, a $30 million sales manufacturer of engine filters.

In 1984, at the age of 40 and with a wife and small children, lifestyle and child-rearing became more important factors in his life. He contacted a San Francisco classmate from HBS and got a job at a software company developing semiconductors. At the time, the Japanese were dumping semiconductors (selling below costs) into the U.S. market. Robert lost his job and went looking for a company to buy. He found a maker of anti-static plastic bags with $7 million in sales and 30 people. He grew sales to $15 million and sold the company.

He started another plastic bag company, Roplast, making a different type of bag for the retail and grocery markets. He remained at his home in Palo Alto but his factory was 200 miles north. He'd do most of his work on computers, visiting the factory for a few days every couple of weeks. In 2006, he began a joint venture with a firm in India to make plastic bags that could compete with the Chinese. Robert said that if ventures like these are to work, there has to be a fundamental trust between partners.

Robert's career shift from large company to small manufacturer was really prompted by a conflict between career and family. "You have to decide," Robert said, as he spoke from his home within walking distance of the Stanford University campus.

FIGHTER TO PEACE KEEPER

Not many HBS graduates chose the military for their primary career, but Vietnam Marine Corps veteran Dave Garner did just that, remaining for a total of 25 years before moving to the private sector. Dave got his MBA and became a budget officer at a logistics base in Georgia for his next four years before being put in charge of the University of Notre Dame's Marine ROTC program from 1975 to 1978. He watched ND's football team win the national championship in 1977. He then taught at the Commander College in Quantico, spent time in Okinawa, Washington, the Newport War College, and Washington again, where he worked under the Joint Chief of Staff for the Marines.

After retiring from the military, Dave moved to a private job with the Logistics Management Institute, a nonprofit organization with 750 professionals that does analysis work for the Defense Department, primarily on national security. After six years there, he spent ten years with NATO. Among his assignments was enforcing the 1995 peace agreement between Bosnia and Croatia. He also explored how the United States should partner with foreign countries to share technological systems. In 1999, Dave went back to Vietnam for two weeks as a tourist. He summarized his career: "I've done what I liked doing."

BANKER TO KINDERGARTEN TEACHER

Madeline Miller became familiar with HBS when her husband was there while she worked as a librarian at Harvard College. When he got his MBA in 1968, she signed on to earn her own degree. An inherently shy person, she called the experience of classroom discussions using case studies "terrifying." As one of the few married women enrolled, this English major with no accounting background felt like an outlier. She made it through to graduate in 1970 and join Boston Safe Deposit and Trust Company, a subsidiary of the Boston Company. She worked on special projects and logistics, and over ten years earned the titles of treasurer and chief financial officer of the parent company.

When her husband took a job in New York City, Madeline moved and joined Merrill Lynch in the treasury area, focusing on internal operations and cash management. After a few years, she became director of banking and funds management. In 1990, however, after ten years of expansion and contraction at Merrill, she was laid off.

"I was embarrassed," she admitted. In hindsight, however, she said it was "a great gift to be laid off." She volunteered in New York City public schools and became a kindergarten teacher. She also took courses and received a master's in education. Following a divorce in 1987, she moved with her daughter to Philadelphia. From 1996 to 2003, she taught kindergarten and first grade classes, initially in the public school system and then at an independent school, which had only 8 to 12 children per class. She retired as a full-time teacher in 2003 after she remarried and decided to travel. She still tutors children in first grade reading.

Madeline shared her observations on teaching, and noted that when she grew up the teacher's word was law. "Parents need to be advocates for their children, but the pendulum has swung too far," she said. She strongly believes that troubled school systems need small classes for effective learning, especially in the early years. She also believes the quality of the principal "makes a huge difference in the culture of the school."

EXPERIMENTING

Jim Coyne's first job out of HBS was for an international engineering and consulting firm. This lasted only nine months. When Jim's father became ill, he was asked to come to Philadelphia and run the family business, which distributed industrial chemicals. He ran it for ten years, expanding into oxygen distribution and alternative energy. He also had time to "experiment with things," including real estate investing and working as an adjunct professor at Wharton for four years.

In 1980, he entered the 97th U.S. Congress as part of the "Reagan Sweep" for Republicans. His opponent in the election had received 70% of the vote in the previous election, but the issues of gasoline rationing and fiscal reform led to Jim's victory. He remembered, "It was a fulfilling time to be a Congressman," even though he was a minority member in the House, since the economy was a focus of much of the legislation. He ran again for a second term in 1982 but lost by 1,000 votes out of 220,000 cast in his new Democrat-drawn district. "Politicians choose their voters rather than voters choose their politicians," was how he described it.

For the next ten years, Jim kept busy on various jobs: special assistant to President Reagan directing private sector initiatives; CEO of the American Consulting Engineers Council; and President of the American Tort Reform Association. The last of these he formed to help restrict litigation against engineers. In 1987, he founded Americans to Limit Congressional Terms with the goal of preventing incumbent members of Congress from using redistricting to assure continuous reelection. This effort raised millions of dollars and got 25 states to approve limits before the U.S. Supreme Court ruled five to four against Congressional term limits.

In 1994, executive recruiter and HBS classmate Len Pfeiffer placed Jim, a pilot, as president of the National Air Transport Association. This organization represented 2,000 companies and had

212

20 employees, and Jim served for 18 years. Jim said the biggest issue he faced was the growth of drones and how to guarantee safety. He pointed out that there are two billion vehicles in the United States, including lawnmowers, elevators, etc., with 99% needing a person at the controls. The CIA projects that in 30 years there will be 50 billion vehicles, with only 5% operated by humans.

Jim also observed that there are now over 22,000 trade associations in Washington, D.C. Instead of fighting with one another, more are working together to negotiate compromise positions before going to Congress. For example, the American Trial Lawyers Association will try to reach agreement with the American Tort Reform Association on certain issues to present a united front. He also noted that national legislation often can't get passed, so some issues are pushed at the state level to achieve legislative reforms.

Jim retired in 2013, but said he flunked retirement. After six months he joined a government relations firm in D.C. to do what he called "creative advocacy." He has two regrets in looking back on his career. "I should have kept a journal/diary at Congress and the White House. I also should have gotten to know better the people I contacted."

A New Team

John Schaefer was a graduate of the Naval Academy who spent four years in the service before attending HBS. He earned the distinction of graduating as a Baker Scholar, and was sent to Washington, D.C., to work first for the Secretary of the Navy and then for the Secretary of Defense. He was one of six classmates fulfilling military obligations in D.C., working on high-level projects while coworkers thought they were civilians. In 1971, John was transferred to the White House, where he worked on moving grain to Russia and also on oil imports to the United States. The 1973 Arab oil embargo led to the creation of the Federal Energy Office. John was assistant administrator in charge of energy allocation. When shortage fears led to long gasoline lines in the United States, it was John's idea to set odd-even license plate days for getting gas.

John was released from the Navy in 1973 and left the White House in 1974, moving to join the Baker Oil Tool Company in California as assistant to the CEO. Over 14 years, he moved up to group VP and was made a board member. In 1987, however, a new CEO fired him because he said "he wanted his own team." John spent the next three years as CEO at Levolor, a manufacturer of venetian blinds that was in default on its loans. Soon, even though sales went from $300 million to $250 million, profits went from a $22 million loss to a $12 million annual gain. He then spent three years with a medical company, which he took public and sold.

Timing on the next CEO assignment wasn't as good. He bought a business that made testing equipment for data components, and took it from $15 million revenue to $190 million in two years. Unfortunately, after he turned down a chance to sell the company, the internet crash of 2000 drove sales down to $20 million. John exited in 2002.

John now invests in multifamily housing and sits on the boards of two public companies. He also travels for pleasure. "I never had aspirations to be CEO of a major public company," he said. "Operating at the top, you can get caught up in tactics and miss the major turns in the road. It's hard to see the big things."

A Winning Performance

For the first 15 years of his career, Dick Cavanagh remained with the same employer but lived the life of a corporate nomad. He joined the prestigious consulting firm McKinsey and Company and started in the Washington, D.C. office, before accepting assignments to Copenhagen, London, and Amsterdam. In each of these cities, he participated on different teams to tackle various consulting projects. Dick explained that McKinsey intentionally mixes locations and team members to prevent an individual from forming a set point of view.

The various assignments were challenging. Two that he is allowed to discuss were (1) dealing with the many U.S. railroad bankruptcies of the early 1970s and (2) trying to keep the air traffic system functioning when President Reagan fired all the traffic controllers after they went on strike. The McKinsey team helped consolidate seven bankrupt railroads into a single insolvent entity and went to work.

First, they convinced the federal government to deregulate pricing, since rates had commonly been based on the value of the cargo shipped, not the size or weight of the shipment or the cost of handling. This allowed the surviving railroad to set rates that would generate a profit. They created so-called certificates of value that were swapped for outstanding debt, so while it took time, the debt holders eventually were made whole without straining the railroad's cash flow. Next, they established an information system that allowed the railroad to keep track of both total employees and total railroad cars. These numbers were new data for management. "It was basic blocking and tackling," Dick said, and it worked.

A similar emphasis on the basics helped solve the air traffic mess. "We convinced the FAA to stop planes from taking off unless they had a place to land. We recommended different lanes in the sky for slow planes and fast planes. We prevented worker shift changes during peak times when the skies were full." Since President Reagan wouldn't allow the workers back once the strike began, retired controllers and military controllers were added to the controllers who hadn't gone on strike to fill the void until new controllers could be trained. In six months, 10% of the former manpower was successfully handling 80% of the original air traffic.

While at McKinsey, Dick also co-authored the best-selling management book titled, "The Winning Performance," which has become a classic. Even with the book, being made a partner at the firm, and participating in so many interesting assignments, Dick felt there was a need for more stability in his life. "The longer you stay at McKinsey, the worse your quality of life becomes," he said. He had taken a leave earlier to spend three years tackling the federal budget during the Carter administration. He saved $12 billion by improving cash management, but failed in an effort to restructure the overall government system for better results. "It's a young person's job to work in government. They have more energy than judgment," he observed. The experience, however, did prepare him for the position of executive dean at Harvard's Kennedy School of Government. He left McKinsey and signed on, spending over 15 years there. He currently serves as a part-time faculty member.

After nine years as executive dean, he left that position to become president and CEO of the Conference Board, at the time an organization helping companies get useful information on business trends. Membership was 90% U.S.-based, and Dick set a goal of going global. He recruited worldwide, reaching 40% of membership from outside the United States. The Conference Board bought the leading economic indicators series from the U.S. government and expanded it to cover 80% of the world's GDP. The company also launched a measurement of consumer confidence and a study of corporate governance to recommend best practices. He continued improving business information and guidance for 13 years before stepping down.

Dick remains active, although he has reduced his board memberships from nine to four. Nonprofit boards he has served on include his alma mater, Wesleyan University; Education Testing Service (five years as chairman); Ashoka, a social enterprise fund; Volunteers of America (chairman); and the Boston Symphony Orchestra. The current most time-consuming position he holds is non-executive chairman of Black Rock Mutual Funds, a position he's had since 2007. During the financial crisis of 2008 and 2009, the conservative investing approach practiced by Black Rock made it the favorite with the Federal Reserve and U.S. Treasury to rescue floundering investment firms needing to sell assets. Black Rock bought such businesses and grew into the largest investment manager in the world with $4.7 trillion in assets, larger than Vanguard and Fidelity funds combined.

When asked what concerns he has overseeing such a huge amount of investor money, he mentioned three things. First, the middle 80% of the U.S. population (excluding the poorest and richest 10% at the bottom and top) is "woefully underinvested for retirement." Second, the high debt levels and concentrated power of both banks and investment bankers are greater even than before the 2008 financial crisis hit. Third, "Wall Street is back to its old tricks again, such as promoting ETFs (exchange-traded funds) built on financial derivatives that are only as solid as the financial counter-party in the transaction." With financial risks growing again, Dick isn't so sure that we're through with panics going forward.

16

FINDING YOUR
SWEET SPOT

HERE ARE MANY REASONS TO seek a new job. You might have to because a new boss wants his own people, or perhaps because you aren't doing what's expected for the position. Maybe the industry or company is in decline, and people must be let go. Often, your family wants more of your time, seldom available because of frequent travels or heavy workloads that you're expected to do. Sometimes a change is prompted simply by your desire to do something "more meaningful" or better suited to your personality. If you've been financially successful in previous positions, it's much easier to make the break for something better. Having accumulated adequate wealth unlocks the way to choose freely what you want to do. This independence of choice, rather than an ability to buy luxurious things, is what motivates many successful business people.

One executive recruiter interviewed estimated that 90% of the people taking jobs "fall into things" rather than map out a strategic plan to get where they want to go. This is true of business graduates of Harvard as well as others. It's not easy envisioning the perfect opportunity when you're starting out, and harder still to know when you have it. The biggest advantage HBS grads may have over others is being both confident and opportunistic. If a job isn't working for whatever reason, it's easier to seek something better when you don't worry as much about personal financial failure. Where you start isn't as important as where you end up when pursuing a career. Often, a decision on what's right for you is made only after trying several things.

A number of people mentioned in this book suggest that those starting a career should follow their passion, not the money trail. To do so, of course, you have to know who you are and what you want. When you look back after 40 years, you should feel good about what happened. This may require four or more job changes, so be ready for them. To assure that you have future job choices, don't train too narrowly, focus and work hard, avoid making enemies, and maintain impeccable ethics and integrity. If you can build a financial cushion, that's great, since it allows you to leave a career track and independently decide how you want to spend your time each day.

The most satisfied HBS graduates seem to be those who look at business opportunities through a wide lens. The job responsibilities are considered first, but one shouldn't overlook the company's culture, family happiness, or personal goals. You should experiment with different tasks while young enough to look elsewhere if you don't find the right thing. Also, be willing to challenge yourself and take career chances. As one graduate said, "I'd much rather be criticized for doing something than not trying to do something."

17

A PERSONAL JOURNEY

I T WAS EARLY SPRING IN 1968, I was at the end of my senior year of college at Princeton University, and I had three potential paths: (1) go into journalism for a year, thus fulfilling a journalism scholarship requirement I had; (2) go to Harvard Business School; or (3) go (or be drafted) into the military. I chose to repay the scholarship, take my chances that I wouldn't be drafted, and told Harvard I was on my way.

About a third of our class came to HBS right from college. Now, virtually nobody gets accepted without some sort of real world experience. That's a good thing, in my opinion. Since I was coming from an all-male college (Princeton later became coed in 1969), I wasn't ready to take full advantage of what HBS had to offer: refining your personal goals, getting to know the professors and what they had to teach, and bonding with fellow classmates. Instead, my arrival in the Boston area presented a very different opportunity. I had 17 dates in my first three months. Studies were still important, but secondary.

To my surprise, classes were fun, and because we used the case discussion method, there was little you could do to study for exams. I thrived on the argumentative give-and-take of classroom discussions with the 94 others in my section. We had the same group for all our first-year classes, so this is where most personal friendships developed.

I remember especially the first class, "Planning in the Business Environment." We had been given a case to study and all of us prepared well, hoping to make a favorable impression early. Professor Raymond asked the simple question, "Who would like to start the class?" At least 50 hands went up and one lucky student was called on. He spent 15 minutes giving what, he thought, was the definitive analysis of the case and how he would solve the problem. When finished, he awaited the applause that never came.

The professor, with a vest covering a stomach that showed too much personal prosperity, simply asked, "Does anybody else have a different opinion?" Forty-nine hands went up, with each person ready to attack the analysis and solution given by the first classmate. This was a shock to him and his personal image, only partly offset by the sky blue Lincoln Continental convertible he drove to classes. Towards the end of the first year, very few students volunteered to begin the case discussions. We quickly learned there were seldom right or wrong answers. Everything seemed gray and subject to different approaches. It was both humbling and confidence-building to know your opinion always counted, but your solution to a problem was rarely the best.

Professors overcame the lack of volunteers with random name-calling to find a discussion starter. This presented major problems for those who hadn't done the six-plus hours of preparation the night before that was usually necessary to deal adequately with the three cases assigned. Like many students, I prepared well for one case, read and thought about the second, and did very little with the third. There were many classes where a student just kept his head down and hoped to avoid notice. For one particularly long and challenging marketing case, I decided to walk in 10 minutes after the class started to avoid being called on. As I entered at the back of the class, the professor looked up and saw me. He said, "Mr. Chokel, perhaps you can start the discussion since your classmates are unable to do so." I declined and sat down, wishing I could disappear.

OUR ENCORE YEAR

My experiences during the second year were much different than the first. Courses were selected, not mandatory. At least three-quarters of the students in each class were people you didn't know. Ties and sport jackets disappeared as dress became more casual. Blue jeans, t-shirts, and loafers were popular. Harvard College across the river was louder, with regular protests against the Vietnam War. After 18 months, I had received a 4-F classification from the Army because of high blood pressure. This did not happen without two physicals at the Boston Army Base, one (during the summer) at the Chicago Army Base, and nine separate visits to the Harvard infirmary to have my blood pressure evaluated. The Army doctor in Chicago accused me of taking drugs to elevate my blood pressure and sent me to a room to give a blood sample. As I was doing this, the orderly said, "It's only 9:10 in the morning and you're already the fifth person he's accused of taking drugs and threatened to send to Leavenworth" (a military prison). Both he and I were not happy. A figurative sword was hanging over many of our heads. But by early 1970, I was no longer eligible for service and could complete my education.

Not so fortunate were about a dozen classmates who had their HBS studies suspended until after their service stints. My intended roommate for the second year was so sure he would be drafted, he chose not to return to HBS. He wasn't drafted and finished HBS in June of 1971. Others went, served their tour of duty, and returned later to finish HBS. Some went into various programs that allowed finishing

HBS before going into the service. These folks generally landed posts in Washington, D.C., after graduation as the war wound down and their talents were put to use in the political/military mix that is D.C.

At the end of our second year, most of Harvard University went on strike to protest against the war, but not the B-School. We just wanted to finish and get on with our lives, although the black HBS students came within one vote of joining the strike. We were also on alert during May, 1970, when it was rumored that Harvard College students were planning to come across the river to our side and "trash" the Business School to protest the "crimes" of the military/industrial complex. We stayed inside with locked doors despite the early warmth of a Boston spring, watching the bridge from Harvard Square for the masses that never came.

While we were closing out the second half of our second year, I was busy with my own issues, getting real-world business experiences far beyond my seven years as a paperboy, two years as a golf caddy, and summer stints as a copyboy at a newspaper, an audit trainee for an accounting firm, and a consultant studying the market for forged metal parts.

How to Make Enemies and $5,000

During the first year, I led a group of five students applying for the HBS franchise for the school's weekly paper, *The HarBus News*. I simply gathered the first-year students who had written regularly for the paper and applied for the right to take over the franchise in the fall of 1969. This franchise generated about $25,000 in annual profits. We won the authorization to run the franchise and split the profits amongst us five. We agreed to different profit percentages depending on our jobs: editor (me), publisher, advertising manager, business manager, and a person to handle "Careers and the MBA," a booklet published just before recruiting of second-year students started. This one-time publication allowed firms looking to hire to write articles such as "Life as a Consultant" or "Banker" or "Manufacturer," etc. The publication didn't take much time and ads sold themselves, but it did generate about 75% of the total *HarBus* profits.

Two major disputes interrupted the harmony of our 1969–70 newspaper efforts. First, the publisher, who was black, wasn't performing the full job he was assigned. I (white) wasn't happy about this, but the three others (white) wanted to fire the publisher for non-performance. When the HBS administrators heard what was going on, I was called into the office of the Dean of Students. He said, "No matter how bad things are, you can't fire the publisher because it will look like a racial dispute." I could see his point. I sat down with the publisher and agreed to do his job along with my own 25-hours-per-week duties as editor for a portion of his share of the profits. He agreed and I kept very busy finishing the term with both my classroom work and my newspaper responsibilities.

Unfortunately, Harvard College's daily and well-known newspaper, *The Harvard Crimson*, found out about this near-revolt and decided to write a story. When it was eventually published, the article was unflattering but accurate. The headline read, "The Har-Bus News–How to Make Enemies and $5,000." I learned a lesson: Avoid giving others a chance to make you look bad. This helps me understand those classmates who were nervous about what might be written about them, and declined to be interviewed for this book.

WATCH THE CASH

The second problem with *The HarBus* became evident just two weeks before school was to end in 1970. We had arranged a meeting for the five proprietors to get our respective share of the profits. As we sat there, our jaws dropped when the business manager reported we had no money. We learned that the person handling "Careers and the MBA," our big revenue generator, had sold ads but made no attempt to collect payments due. He announced that only he knew who owed what, and he didn't intend to collect anything unless we gave him a larger split of the profits than was originally negotiated.

The meeting almost ended in a physical brawl, but I asked that the individual who was blackmailing us to step out of the room while the rest of us discussed his profit revision proposal. After some choice words were expressed, I asked the others if someone could stay in Boston for the summer and collect the advertising revenue due as best he could. We all had plans. I then said we should accept the revisions of profits since there wasn't much else we could do. We had not allowed for a Plan B.

Eventually, we all collected our shares based on the new money allocation. Since that day, four of us have been good friends, brought closer together by adversity. The fifth, who subsequently boasted how he played hardball with us and backed us into a corner, hasn't attended an HBS reunion (to the best of my knowledge). Tactics like he used tend to be heard about and frowned on by at least most of the class. He hurt his reputation, and I learned a valuable, first-hand lesson on the value of monitoring and controlling the cash.

OFF TO A SLOW START

After graduation from HBS, I made some career moves that displeased my father, the president of a small market research firm he owned. In hindsight, these moves weren't very smart. I did no interviewing on campus and turned down offers from the two companies I had worked for in the previous two summers: one offer from a large accounting firm to work anywhere in the world and a second offer from a Chicago management consulting firm. I was ready for a break after four rigorous years at Princeton and two challenging years at Harvard. I didn't have much money but thought there was enough to spend a year hitchhiking around the world. Not a good idea when launching a business career. No wonder HBS almost never takes students straight from college anymore.

226

I did in fact fly to Europe in June of 1970, missing the HBS graduation ceremony. My girlfriend, now my wife of 46 years, met me in Amsterdam and we spent 2½ months wandering the continent as we hitchhiked, not sure where we'd be each night. In mid-August, she flew back to the United States to get a master's degree in public health. I continued on alone, first to Spain, then across southern France and Italy, down the coast of the former Yugoslavia, into Greece, and eventually, by early October, to Istanbul. At that point it was getting cold, the students I was meeting along the way had disappeared, I had a virus that I couldn't shake, and the next leg of the trip was across Turkey to Afghanistan. I decided to head back to the United States.

I flew to Pittsburgh, where my girlfriend was attending school, and took a part-time job advising people on personal finances. This job included selling life insurance and mutual funds as well as advising on taxes and estate planning. I earned little but learned a lot. At Christmas, I proposed to my girlfriend and we planned to be married in September 1971. It was time to get serious about earning a living.

A BUSINESS REBIRTH

My father had a small market and public opinion survey company in Cleveland that did studies for large corporations, politicians, and public utilities trying to judge the mood of employees, customers, or the general public. He wanted me to join him and eventually take over the firm. The studies were interesting but my two years working there were difficult. With only nine full-time employees, one a partner who supervised about 500 part-time interviewers, I had a job and a desk but limited opportunity to add value. Major decisions were made by my father, and the others knew what needed to be done far better than I. I did what I could to stay busy, but felt like a fish out of water. During those two years, I did not advance my corporate skills and felt reborn when I left the firm for a job with a large Cleveland bank.

I joined the bank as an internal marketing analyst and economist. The bank was Union Commerce, a "go-go" bank in the early '70s, led by two former Citicorp executives from New York City. There were several young Harvard MBAs working there. My start-date was a hot and humid day in August 1973, and the bank's large lobby in Cleveland was not air-conditioned. I showed up in a suit but by 10:00 a.m., had taken my jacket off. My boss came over to my desk and loomed over me. He told me to put the jacket back on since I was visible to our public customers. That afternoon, I sat at my desk and watched the sweat run down my nose and onto my desk, getting nothing done. To this day, I'm convinced that air conditioning represents one of the most important changes in banking.

A lack of familiarity with banking prevented me from realizing that in late 1973, four months after I had joined, the bank was burdened by overly-aggressive real estate lending. A final blowout was a mid-December black-tie party in the bank's lobby with open-bar (adjacent but not on the bank premises) and multiple bands for all employees and their spouses/dates. My boss, staff assistant to the CEO, was not well-liked in the bank because of his role running quarterly performance reviews of the managers. He came in Monday morning and found that a plate of spareribs with sauce had been dumped into one of his desk drawers. By January, major layoffs began as the bank desperately began to cut costs.

My new job was doing an internal consulting project with five others to improve all areas of the bank. We answered to the bank's new CEO and spent six months analyzing just about everything. We made recommendations that were well received and implemented. I was rewarded by being allowed into commercial lending after three months of credit training.

Life as a Lending Officer

I was assigned to the prestigious post of lending to large Cleveland companies, one of which was Standard Oil of Ohio. At the time (1975), Sohio was running the major oil discovery in Prudhoe Bay, Alaska, but needed to build a pipeline to get the oil out. British Petroleum agreed to pay for the pipeline in return for getting increasing ownership of Sohio as more oil was moved and sold. The idea was that eventually BP would own a majority of Sohio.

We bankers were regularly called to New York City where 40 to 50 of us would gather to hear the Sohio treasurer report on what progress was being made. Despite his youth, he was always well prepared and very professional. At the end of the presentation he asked for questions. I generally was the only one who had any questions. Afterwards, he would come up to me and thank me for the questions, saying after all his preparation it was nice to know somebody was paying attention. A few years later, the British government was going to divest its BP stockholdings in a major sale. I suggested to Sohio's treasurer that his banks might finance the purchase of the BP shares. I considered this a great move, since eventually BP would control Sohio, but effectively Sohio would control BP. This path was considered, but political complications prevented further action.

Another customer I had was a large coal company. It gathered its bankers for a meeting and a visit to its Kentucky operations. A field trip was scheduled to tour an underground mine. I wore a suit, white shirt, and dress shoes that day, as did half the bankers. The rest wore jeans and sweat shirts. We quickly learned which bankers had experience lending to coal mines.

For two years, I had fun lending to large companies, but this required little credit skill and mainly involved going to meetings with lots of other bankers and pretending your bank's share of the loan was important. Then one of my bank superiors asked me to move into the small business lending unit with the intention of taking charge after a short period of time. In my mind this was a downward move, going down in size from $10 million loans to $500,000 or less loans, but he explained it was important for me as a "rising star" to take the job and dispel the common opinion that small business lending was not important.

I loved lending to small businesses, and eventually had six officers and three support people reporting to me. My credit skills were sharpened and I enjoyed the business owners I dealt with. After two years doing this, however, my superiors decided that small businesses should be handled out of the branches despite my protests that their owners liked to be close to the power-makers in the main office. I was told to rent an office near a branch and relocate myself. That same day, I sent out my resume to several financial institutions, and dragged my feet in relocating because I didn't want to saddle my successor with an office that might not be desirable.

After three weeks, my immediate boss asked why I hadn't found a new office and I was honest and told him I was looking for another job. Big mistake! He sympathized with me but felt compelled to tell his boss, who called me to his office immediately and told me to pack up my desk that day. I refused, saying I was finishing work for some current customers and leaving suddenly would make it appear that I'd done something wrong. He asked how long I would need and I said three weeks, so he said not to say anything and prepare for my departure. It was an uncomfortable three weeks, but I left and moved to a competitor across the street.

A SLIPPERY SLIDE DOWN THE OIL PATCH

The new bank hired me to replace someone who had retired four months earlier. I was to lend to large companies again. Unfortunately, other loan officers had taken over various pieces of the retiring officer's portfolio, and I had a desk but virtually no accounts. No problem — I simply started calling on various smaller Cleveland companies saying we were interested in their businesses and asking to meet with the owner, president, or chief financial officer. I was then working for Cleveland Trust, the largest and most prestigious bank in Ohio, and it had always expected potential customers to call when needing something. My initiating calls won lots of invitations to visit and several requests for new loans. I earned a reputation as a go-getter in the bank. My only problem was I called on one company whose owner's father remembered my bank demanding immediate payment of his loan during the Depression. I retreated with lots of apologies.

After two years of building my own portfolio, I was asked to take charge of the specialized energy lending group in 1981, a hot time in the oil patch. The bank hired a petroleum engineer to judge the value of reserves, and together we traveled around Ohio, where lots of smaller wells were being drilled, and eventually went looking for borrowers in Denver, Houston, Michigan, West Virginia, and other oil patch areas. Our portfolio grew to over $100 million despite the conservative approach of our petroleum engineer. I took as collateral farmland, personal guarantees, and whatever I could to justify some loans that our petroleum engineer wouldn't agree to with only energy reserves as collateral. There were a lot of aggressive energy partnership salesmen and promoters in the oil business at the time, many not honest, but it was very difficult to identify the dishonest ones.

In mid-1985, oil was $35 per barrel "on its way to $100" according to some projections, and the Texas banks were all very aggressive in their lending practices. We pulled back on our lending. When I was asked how much I could grow the portfolio in 1986, I said I'd be lucky to keep overall loans constant, making new loans only to replace those being paid back. Since senior management had just negotiated with First City of Houston to share in their loans, I was told only 25% or more loan growth was acceptable. The first two First City loan deals we were shown were awful, and I turned them down. I prepared my successor to take over and announced I would be leaving at year's end.

In late 1985, oil lending was very dangerous. I knew that I could get loan growth of 25% or even 50%, but there was a high probability the loans would go bad. I wasn't going to be blamed for doing things that hurt the bank despite what my superiors wanted. I stepped away without having a job in the wings, although I did have a working spouse.

Four months after I left, the price of oil went from $35 to $10 per barrel, and in 1986, the large Texas banks all went out of business. My bank suffered relatively minor oil lending losses. It did, however, eventually run into trouble because it acquired a Denver bank and that bank had a heavy concentration of energy lending. Soon, my bank would be merged into Society Bank, a stronger Cleveland bank.

SMALL-TIME VENTURE CAPITALIST

In 1986, at the age of 40 with two young children, I was unemployed but ready to start a firm to invest in small companies with good ideas in the Cleveland area. After six months trying to gather investors to join me, I decided there were too many different ideas to form a group, so I chose to try this on my own. For the next 20 years, I drew no paycheck, making ends meet by successfully investing in the public stock market. I did manage to invest relatively small amounts in 30 private companies, most of them startups or very small firms. It was easy making the investments, but very hard getting the money back.

I had a few successes, but very few. Looking back, I would not advise this as a career path. Some companies failed because the product didn't prove as good as anticipated. Most failed because the entrepreneur had too much ego to accept guidance, or ran the business in a poor fashion. As a minority investor I tried to guide, not dictate. The companies that tried but failed and shut down, I learned to respect. It was the firms that got close to success before doing something stupid and failing that bothered me. If I had it to do over again, I would invest only if I could take charge if things weren't working out.

Among the failures there were many lessons to learn. I put money into a technically bankrupt business, a Sotheby's-type auction house, and helped make it successful. The entrepreneur then tried to play in a more national market with less concern paid to the art consignors, and eventually the firm ran out of money. In another situation, a manufacturer knew that the federal government was requiring double-walled storage tanks under all gasoline stations and ramped up to supply them. When federal implementation of the new rules was delayed, a large inventory of tanks drained the company of cash and forced a shutdown.

A maker of synthetic marijuana (THC) to alleviate nausea in chemo patients almost had a German firm lined up to make it and an American firm lined up to sell it. Government controls proved too burdensome, however, so both firms dropped out. The entrepreneur morphed into a Chinese pharmaceutical company making IV-solution bags by cashing in a favor owed to him by the Chinese. He bought the operation's factory and then learned that the large hospitals that were customers were all run by the Chinese military, which didn't pay the government company making the IV-solution bags. They also didn't pay him when he took the operation over. He complained and was given instead the rights to bottle soft drinks at a Beijing-area factory, what he called a "license to print money." This new venture seemed promising until Coke and Pepsi cut prices to prevent him from getting a foothold.

Equity I put into Ohio's first minority-owned investment bank seemed to work initially, but soon the large fees gained from underwriting municipal bonds had to be used primarily to buy the business from politicians and other investment firms. The idea of "pay to play" was too costly for the firm, and it was forced to sell out.

Perhaps the strangest investment was in a small startup, which would make and sell a lightweight concrete mix that had specialized uses and could even float a concrete canoe. For four years, I was one of a dozen investors who poured money into the company. It was always on the verge of success, which never seemed to happen.

Eventually, we determined that the entrepreneur was misleading us to get more money and we brought in a new CEO and fired the entrepreneur. He sued us for not giving him enough money to allow him to be successful. We won the lawsuit after a ten-week jury trial, but our lawyer cost $700,000, which the firm paid because the bylaws indemnified us as directors and officers. Since the firm had no money, we had to lend the $700,000 for the firm to pay the legal bills. Ouch! Remarkably, the new CEO brought in cleaned up this mess by dropping the lightweight concrete product and focusing on a more mundane product to start making money and repay our loans. When this was done, many of the investors sold their stock to the new CEO for $1. I remained with my original investment and several years later actually made a profit in selling my shares to the CEO.

RUNNING A COMPANY

In 1988, my wife joined me in retirement to raise a third child and spend more time with our first two children. Soon after, my stockbroker mentioned to me that another of his clients had found a bankrupt manufacturing business in Cleveland that was for sale. I was introduced to the other client and agreed to invest in the Cleveland Vibrator Company, with my partners being two engineers who then were working for a larger company. They would be active in management and I would be a passive investor, with each of us owning a third of this 35-employee company.

A bank was liquidating Cleveland Vibrator, a maker of industrial vibrators for material handling, so we had to move fast before it completely disappeared. We each were to put in $100,000 of equity and the company would get a loan from the Small Business Administration (SBA) for $800,000. When the SBA said that any shareholder with 20% or more in equity would have to personally guarantee the $800,000 loan, I reduced my ownership to 19.9% but got an option to buy shares from my partners to get me eventually to a one-third ownership position. Since the SBA could collect the whole $800,000 from any of us and I was the deepest pocket and was not going to be active in the business, this was the only prudent way for me to get the deal done.

Two days before closing, both my partners said they could only find $50,000 in cash, or half what they had promised to contribute. I had to lend them each $50,000 to get the deal completed, but at least I wasn't guaranteeing the SBA loan. Two years later, the company looked like it would return to bankruptcy. My partners ran this small company like a large company, with all the executive perks that so many large company managers believe themselves entitled to receive. They each had company cars and bulky cell phones, and traveled to Orlando with spouses and attended conferences for small businesses. I sat them down and said I would save the company, but only if they would sell me a controlling interest. If not, I would deal with the bank when the company defaulted on the loan and would eventually own 100%. They agreed there was wisdom in my first suggestion.

In my new role as CEO, I spent only about six hours a week at the company. While there, I pursued two objectives: (1) convincing senior management that they, not the owners, should make the decisions; and (2) cutting all unnecessary expenditures. Out went the corporate cars, the *Wall Street Journal* subscription, corporate charity gifts, and even our salaries. We owners would not make anything until the company did. We were all welcome at the company, but would not be paid anything beyond our share of the earnings. We also reviewed our major suppliers and sought price reductions or other supply sources. One easy target was a lawsuit the company had initiated, which was costing us $35,000 a year in legal fees. I reviewed correspondence and saw that we were chasing a former employee who had started a competitive operation with our drawings, plans, etc. His lawyer had written us, "Can you prove" that the drawings, plans, etc. were yours in the first place? We couldn't, so we stopped the legal drain.

With the cost-cutting and long-time senior managers making daily decisions they thought were best for the company, we became profitable in four months. In a year, we began paying bonuses. In five years, we had prepaid our seven-year SBA loan and began to pay large bonuses to non-owner employees equivalent to 20% of pretax earnings. We have been consistently profitable every year since. As an inner-city manufacturer in the rust belt with a very diverse work-force, it's a great feeling to be successful and to be selling 15-20% of your products outside North America.

A Different Approach

Looking at my post-banking career investing in small companies, I have to admit that I probably should not have made such invest-ments unless I was able to take control if things went off course. People change a lot with success, and they can change even more when desperate. People who are honest in prosperous times can become dishonest if pressed against the wall. One entrepreneur I knew for 20 years and had financially backed called me one day and said he needed a short-term loan to help his company bridge a cash shortfall. I lent the company the money, which he promptly transferred (without my knowledge) to a different company run by his brother that couldn't make payroll. His brother's company went bankrupt, and so did his. I recovered very little of my money.

After having headaches and disappointments for almost 20 years, I finally joined an angel investor group with 98 others to make investments in startups. The screening we did for these investments was more thorough, the documentation more complete, and the sums involved larger, generally $250,000 plus our individual side-car investments. Once again, however, the entrepreneurs went every which way once they had the money, and the jury is still out on whether overall these investments will be successful. At least the workload of chasing the entrepreneurs and trying to guide them is being shared by the group. If you want to invest in small companies, my suggestion is to take charge from the beginning so you can force needed change and not rely on persuasion after the fact.

Investing in public firms has been much more profitable for me. With the internet, you can listen in on quarterly conference calls and review press releases and corporate filings on a daily basis. The more you read about and pay attention to a company, the more success you have as an investor. Can't take the time to follow individual companies? Better that you invest in a low-cost Vanguard fund or another low-cost alternative, since these beat most financial advisors and brokers regularly after fees are considered.

SWINGS AND MISSES

Over my 40 years of public market investing, I've generally tried for home runs, and struck out a lot because of that approach. I'm now especially adverse to companies dependent on government policies that can change overnight. For example, a major landfill company lined all its waste dumps at great expense after a new federal rule forcing all its competitors to do the same as of a certain date. Many of these landfills, however, were owned by municipalities, and when they pleaded poverty, the rule was withdrawn. The better-prepared operator I had invested in wound up going bankrupt when the anticipated increase in business never came.

The most important thing an investor can do is assess the quality of management in a company, especially how oriented the CEO is (or isn't) to shareholder interest. One large, public supermarket chain (First National Supermarkets) went from "promising' to "no upside" for the stock price when its management arranged a leveraged buyout of the firm from all other shareholders. The firm had—over the previous two years—settled a price-fixing lawsuit by issuing coupons to customers allowing $1 off future purchases every six months for three years. It wrote off more than $10 million in costs for this immediately rather than spreading it out over three years. The earnings and stock dropped precipitously.

It further damaged its income statement by undergoing a major remodeling program and a major expansion with new stores. Only later did I discover that it takes six to nine months for a remodeled store to get back to normal because of the dust and confusion of remodeling. A new store requires about 18 months to reach break-even profits since it must win new customers. Management knew the worst was past and the best coming when it bought the company from its public shareholders. To me, this is insider trading at its worst, but such tactics are rarely punished. Know the character of the people you're dealing with is the best advice.

THE WONDER OF TEN-BAGGERS

A half dozen "ten-baggers" made a big difference in my total wealth. These companies returned ten times or more what my initial investment was, and each had its own story. The first was a private manufacturing company that I learned about early in my banking career. I helped the CEO borrow to buy out the company's founder. When I later left the bank, he asked if I would be interested in buying some shares from another shareholder. I made the investment at about four times earnings, and the CEO soon was increasing earnings annually. Every time an investor wanted to sell, I was the most willing to buy since I had confidence in the CEO. The firm eventually sold to a large conglomerate, making me a lot of money. A second private company success was Cleveland Vibrator, bought out of bankruptcy and then turned profitable with me as part-time CEO. Being fair with customers and employees, keeping a tight watch on expenses, and focusing on what must be done created the formula for success.

In the public market, my biggest success was the 1978 purchase of shares in Telecommunications, destined to become the largest cable company in the world under CEO John Malone. I first encountered cable television as a bank lender when asked to consider a loan to a private cable company in Kentucky. I saw negative earnings and negative net worth, and was ready to turn down the loan until my boss told me to spend a few days with the chief operating officer taking a closer look at the business. The COO explained that the red ink was really caused by depreciating all the construction costs over five years, even though the wires, poles, electronics, etc. would last for 20 or more. When the depreciation reached 100% of original cost, the depreciation would end and the profits would be shown.

When I made the loan, I asked what public cable company the COO would recommend as a good investment. He suggested Telecommunications, so I bought and held on as its expansion sent the stock soaring. About 20 years later, after adjusting for splits, my holdings had gone up 100 times in value. At this point, AT&T bought the firm. The conservative AT&T was a big philosophical difference from the go-go Telecommunications, but I was happy to sit on my winnings and collect dividends. Three years later, however, AT&T was down 50% and my 100 times investment return had become 50 times. Don't assume that what some call "safe" stocks are correctly characterized by the market!

An unanticipated winner also came in 1978 when my stockbroker suggested I look into the stock of Charter One Financial, which was converting from a mutual bank structure (owned by depositors) to public stock ownership. I studied the offering circular and saw that the $8 offering price, after investment banking fees, would generate $7.50 per share net to the company, which already was earning about $1 per share even before this new money was received. I wondered how much more the company could earn with the new cash. I bought aggressively. A month later, the stock was down to

$7 per share since small financial firms were thought, at the time, to be too risky. I bought some more. Six years later, I had earned ten times on my investment, largely because the CEO proved very capable. Since the firm's trading symbol was "COFI," I bought ten bags of specialty coffees, stapled them on a poster board, and presented them to the CEO with the inscription: "Congratulations—COFI 10-bagger!"

The company's stock continued to soar, reaching 25 times my original investment, not counting the regular dividends paid out. I met the CEO at a breakfast meeting and congratulated him on his fine performance. He surprised me by saying he didn't like that other financial firms were doing crazy lending in the mortgage market, and these concerns had prompted him to sell all his financial stocks except Charter One. Two weeks later, in 2004, shortly before the housing market crash began, I read the announcement that Charter One had been sold to the U.S. subsidiary of the Royal Bank of Scotland. I should have seen it coming. Reluctantly, I turned over the shares of this wonderful performer and moved on. Finding a small gem of a company early on is a wonderful thing!

Another stock recommended by my broker was a small manufacturing firm in the Cleveland area that was losing money and seemed on the verge of going into bankruptcy. Normally, I would not have been interested, but my broker introduced me to the new CEO brought in to run the firm, with the founder and former-CEO taking a secondary role. The new CEO was very good at asking questions of employees that went to the heart of what was going on, leaving no room for excuses or sloppy answers. He dropped one product line and built up another. The founder disagreed, was out-voted by his board of directors, and then committed suicide. The firm, however, soon improved and increased its value more than ten-fold.

SOUTH OF THE BORDER

Investing in risky stocks is not for the faint of heart. One of my biggest winners was Telefonos de Mexico, the telephone company of Mexico that in 1986 was selling at about 25% of book value and about five times earnings. It was difficult to judge the numbers since the annual report was in Spanish and the accounting not clear. John Templeton, one of the early legends in international investing, had mentioned the stock positively in an article I had read.

When I first bought shares, they were selling for 12.5 cents each and paying 25% in stock dividends each year. I had just left the banking business, had no paycheck, a reasonable savings amount, and a working spouse. I moved my entire 401K plan money from the bank to a self-directed IRA and put all that money into "Tfony," which was the Mexican telephone company's market symbol. The next 18 months were fun as I watched the stock move up a penny here, a penny there. I suspect I became the largest U.S. individual investor, or close to it. At the end of the summer in 1987, the stock approached $1 per share. The crash of October, 1987 brought me back to earth as the stock dropped back to 12.5 cents. I didn't sell on the way up or the way down. Fortunately, in another 18 months it was again pushing $1. I sold and watched it move to $3.50 per share. My reason for investing early on was simple. I believed Mexico would become a major U.S. problem if we didn't help its struggling economy. This observation was accurate then and is accurate still.

CAREER CHOICES

My 12 years working at two different Cleveland banks offered great training and a wonderful opportunity to enjoy conversations and friendships with my fellow employees. What wasn't so good was that in both banks, like in many large companies, your career path leads to different internal jobs and different bosses. Sooner or later, you report to someone whose expectations, personality, morals, intelligence, or concern for your well-being are not what you appreciate. At that point, you keep your head down, try not to make waves, and seek other opportunities: internal or external.

Investing in small companies was personally interesting, but much more difficult and time-consuming than I had imagined. All of the investments I made involved minority ownership positions. I counted on being able to judge the character of the entrepreneur, since the small size of my contributed dollars made it difficult to properly lawyer an arrangement providing investor protection. I also anticipated being able to nudge people in the right directions if things weren't going well. Not so. My advice is to only invest if you can legally replace the founder if the company is failing. Of course, this also means you need to prepare for personally becoming involved in active management if change is necessary. Not a career choice for the faint-hearted!

THE PAIN OF LAWSUITS

Investing in the public markets requires a willingness to read all you can about a particular company, evaluate the quality of management, balance risk vs. reward, and evaluate trends that might be positive or negative. You also must constantly be on the look-out for actions management may take that are very much against shareholder interests. Sometimes these actions result in lawsuits, with a small sum generally awarded to the damaged shareholders.

In two public company lawsuit situations I personally was involved in, the sums eventually awarded weren't so small, but the battle for fairness was very painful. The first of these battles involved a company called First National Supermarkets, whose managers decided to take it private in 1986. I mentioned earlier how actions taken drove the stock price down before the management buyout. I sued under Massachusetts law (where the company was domiciled) to ask the court to determine fair value of my shares. There was a "fairness opinion" offered by a Wall Street firm on the valuation, but this firm received a small fee for this opinion but a very large fee and a piece of the action for helping management do the buyout.

Lawyers who are friendly to you will try to avoid getting involved in lawsuits. That's good advice. I was naïve about how lawyers and the law work. First, pursuing a dissenter's rights proceeding was only possible if you didn't accept management's buyout offer. This meant my money was tied up—in my case, for ten years of litigation. Second, the company's lawyers pursued a common tactic in big company/small individual litigation: bury the small guy in costs. I needed to pay out-of-pocket for my lawyer and they could use the company funds, so they would extend the lawsuit however they could. Third, Massachusetts apparently doesn't believe business disputes should take up the court's valuable time, and so kept pushing us to settle even though the company had no interest in doing so. Finally, my lawyer told me how the law was supposed to work, not how it did work. I was entitled to all relevant information from the company, but many pertinent facts were not given without repeated requests and orders from the court. All of this was expensive and time-consuming.

After ten costly years and much personal time spent on my part to keep legal costs down, I was told I "won the lawsuit" and was awarded more than other shareholders received and 12% compound interest from the date the company went private (since that rate was available for investors at the time). Although I received three times the money I was originally offered, I had to battle for a decade and pay legal fees amounting to much of the gain. The general market rise during those same ten years was more than three times. Despite my personal pain when litigating, I was more troubled that shareholders never knew how management had used, in my opinion, inside information to buy the company at a low price.

SMARTER THE SECOND TIME AROUND

I filed a similar lawsuit about ten years later against Genzyme, a major biological firm based in Cambridge, Massachusetts, that has since been bought by Sanofi. The situation began in December of 2000 when Genzyme bought a company called Biomatrix and combined it with two other company units to form Genzyme Biosurgery. This company was taken public as a tracking stock, where it would have its own shareholders that might benefit from its success but officially was controlled by Genzyme. The company went public at $12, but steadily declined into 2003. While its original product (Synvisc) was doing well, Genzyme Biosurgery was given cancer research to do by Genzyme that generated little if any revenue and caused significant losses. In the spring of 2003, the stock price was around $2 per share.

On May 7, 2003, the stock was selling at $2.57. The next day, Genzyme announced it was buying all the tracking stock back from shareholders for $1.77 per share. Genzyme was allowed to do so since Genzyme Biosurgery's bylaws allowed a forced buyback if the price was 25% over the previous 20-day average closing price. Genzyme Biosurgery had just issued favorable earnings, which prompted the move up to $2.57, but the 20-day average price was lower. I argued that this was unfair and that Genzyme had driven the stock down with the cancer research expenditures and then bought it back knowing favorable earnings had been released. It used the 20-day average to take advantage of setting the lower price paid to shareholders.

In this litigation, I was smarter in deciding upfront I wouldn't fight this on my own. I convinced a class action lawyer in California to take the case on a contingency. He took depositions and filed in the state court system in Massachusetts. He lost with the explanation that the bylaws permitted what was done, without apparent consideration of how it was done. The decision was appealed and we won, but we lost once again at the Supreme Court level in

Massachusetts. My interpretation was that you cannot successfully fight a large state employer in its home state.

Fortunately, a larger and angrier institutional shareholder had filed a similar suit against Genzyme in federal court in New York. This one was viewed more seriously and was allowed to get internal documents and depositions that showed the Genzyme board had discussed much higher internal valuations for Genzyme Biosurgery, but had waited until the stock declined further before triggering the buyback. The key points argued were insider trading, market manipulation, and breach of fiduciary duty by the directors.

Unfortunately, just before the case went to trial, the lawyers in the federal case, who were working on a partial contingency basis, decided to settle rather than risk a trial. All shareholders were awarded $1.58 per share, or a total of $64 million, in addition to the $1.77 originally paid. The institutional investor who initiated the federal case felt strongly the decision should have added at least $10 per share, and probably more, since this was such a blatant attempt to exploit shareholders. The lawyers, however, represented all shareholders and were unwilling to fight the battle during a trial.

The lessons learned from the above two lawsuits are several. Don't believe the law works the way a common-sense business person thinks it should work. Just as lawyers often have problems being business people, business people should not pretend they understand laws. It is very important for anyone engaging a lawyer to understand upfront what really could happen in any court dispute, personal or business. Don't be reluctant to walk away from a clear injustice. In court, things usually get very cloudy. Fighting back, even when winning, can be painful and often unrewarding. Also, don't assume large companies are shareholder-friendly. This is one reason why stagnant or declining stock prices should prompt an early sale, especially if the integrity of the company's leaders is unknown.

I spent two years in classes with many to-be corporate leaders at HBS. I would estimate 20% can be trusted to always do the right thing. Another 20% viewed business as a game, played by getting away with anything you can. The remaining 60% of us fall somewhere in the middle. Harvard Business School has made an effort to judge the ethics of the students accepted and add to their sense of responsibility while they are students, but nobody can anticipate a person's reaction in all cases, especially under stress.

As I look back on my business career, much of my learning was on the job, not in the classroom. That raises the question of whether paying tuition of $75,000 annually plus books and room and board to attend HBS, and sacrificing perhaps $100,000 annually in salary for two years of schooling, is worthwhile. Certainly, HBS grads do well financially. Is that because we were well selected in the admissions process, or well taught by classmates and professors at the school? Perhaps the biggest advantage graduates carry is their HBS alumna/us designation, which opens doors, broadens contacts, and generally gives credibility that the person holding it is intelligent and capable.

There are times when I imagine HBS credentials are an impediment to success. Having made the financial commitment to get an MBA, it is hard to refuse an over-$125,000 starting salary offer, by itself a confirmation that you're a success. Establishing your own company as an entrepreneur right out of school requires a great deal of confidence and courage. It also requires the ability to accept the surprise blows of running a business without crumbling yourself. Ultimately, the ideal goal is to be in charge of your own life and not be financially dependent on others. This goal can be achieved more quickly in an independent effort than within a large corporation where people are competing to move up. Nevertheless, the risks are great in not taking a paying job, which is why so many graduates seem to work for someone else before moving out on their own. The surprise is not so much that they make this choice, but that today approximately 9% of all HBS graduates move directly into working with startups after graduation.

Interview Index

Interview Index